How To Hug A
smelly Guy

Stories of *Hope* for the Broken
who are Serving the Shattered

Jeff Johnson

WestBow
PRESS
A DIVISION OF THOMAS NELSON

WestBow Press books may be ordered through booksellers or by contacting:

WestBow Press
A Division of Thomas Nelson
1663 Liberty Drive
Bloomington, IN 47403
www.westbowpress.com
1-(866) 928-1240

Because of the dynamic nature of the Internet, any web addresses or links contained in this book may have changed since publication and may no longer be valid. The views expressed in this work are solely those of the author and do not necessarily reflect the views of the publisher, and the publisher hereby disclaims any responsibility for them.

Any people depicted in stock imagery provided by Thinkstock are models, and such images are being used for illustrative purposes only.

Certain stock imagery © Thinkstock.

ISBN: 978-1-4497-5227-9 (e)
ISBN: 978-1-4497-5228-6 (sc)
ISBN: 978-1-4497-5229-3 (hc)

Library of Congress Control Number: 2012908537

Printed in the United States of America

WestBow Press rev. date: 08/08/2012

Contents

*P*lease allow me to dedicate this book as a thank you to everyone who is actively involved in the ministry of serving in the city. Urban ministry is more difficult than can be imagined by the outsider, and offers less of the "perks" that can help smooth out the tough spots.

The stories in this piece are poor representations of the vast expanse of ministry that is done every day by people like you. Thanks for sticking it out. It would be an impossible battle if I was in it alone.

Jeff

Acknowledgements

*I*f I start to acknowledge people, I will miss most. As you can tell from the stories, which are a sort of acknowledgement, themselves, there have been people all along the way. Still, I have to at least say thank you:

To Dad, Mom, Phillip, Kathy and Kim who helped form me from the beginning and continue to help me "keep it real."

To Terri, who would weep when others didn't get me and stand with me anyway.

To Luke, Nicholas, Noah and Aaron. If all I ever accomplished in my life was the four of you . . . I'm good.

To Brian, it has been a quite a journey, brother.

To Deb who has pushed, pulled, advised and cajoled—in the nicest possible way.

To Lesa Hess, Mark Eddy Smith and Deborah Breitman for their writing and editorial support.

To the staff at Building Hope in the City and Trinity Church who lost me, at least in part, during the process of writing.

Prologue

*W*hen was the last time you hugged a smelly guy? You know who I mean—you can tell he's coming before he arrives. Maybe the guy's been homeless for a while, living outside, hasn't had a shower in weeks. You smile at him, talk to him politely, ask how he's been, and then he holds up his arms for a hug. What are you going to do? Will you stick out your hand for a shake, maybe pat his shoulder, knowing he'll feel awkward, unwanted, and unclean? Or will you embrace him as a brother, so hard that some of his stink rubs off on you? You can always tell when you've successfully hugged a smelly guy, because his smell will linger on you long after he leaves.

Of course, smelly guys come in different forms. Sometimes they're smelly girls. Sometimes you can't tell they're smelly with your nose. There are people who are emotionally, mentally, or even spiritually smelly. They come in a wide variety of shapes and sizes, but the question remains: When was the last time you hugged a smelly guy so hard you got some on you?

According to the New Testament, the world would describe the church by saying: Look how they love one another, how they care for one another. Look how they get into each other's business without being judgmental. But if your church or community is anything like mine, then it is in fact filled with smelly people. I have people with issues. There are people who ooze with sores and brokenness. There are scores of people who, if you get too close, will end up getting some on you. I mean really, Paul was kidding about that "holy kiss," right?

But look at how the church is called to submit to one another, bear with each other, and forgive whatever grievances we may have against one another. We're called to:

Wash one another's feet (John 13:14);
Love one another (John 13:3; 15:12, 17);
In honor prefer one another (Romans 12:10);
Not judge one another (Romans 14:13);
Receive one another (Romans 15:7);
Salute one another (Romans 16:16);
Greet one another (I Corinthians 16:20; I Peter 5:14);
Serve one another (Galatians 5:13);
Not envy one another (Galatians 5:26);
Bear one another's burdens (Galatians 6:2);
Forbear one another in love (Ephesians 4:2);
Forgive one another (Ephesians 4:32; Col. 3:13);
Teach and admonish one another (Colossians 3:16);
Comfort one another (I Thessalonians 4:18);
Edify one another (I Thessalonians 5:11);
Exhort one another (Hebrews 3:13; 10:25); and
Consider how to provoke one another to love and good works (Hebrews 10:24).

The church, in its truest form, is a one-another church. At their best, God's people are about the business of embracing a broken and smelly world.

Trouble is we don't like this whole "hugging smelly people" thing, do we?

Koinonia (fellowship; intimate community) was an important word to both John and Paul (the saints, not the singers), but it was never used in a merely secular sense. Whereas the people we are willing to hug are usually like us in some fashion, the idea of fellowship founded upon common interests, the physical ties of family, or merely the fact that we root for the same basketball team, has nothing to do with what the apostles meant by koinonia.

In the New Testament, believers can have fellowship on a horizontal plane only because they first have a vertical relationship with God through His Son, the Lord Jesus. The NEB (New English

Bible) translates I John 1:3 as, "what we have seen and heard we declare to you, so that you and we together may share in a common life, that life which we share with the Father and with His Son, Jesus Christ."

Vertically, our relationship with God covers us in His blood. In our relationships horizontally, we are called to share just as intimately, just as completely, but that's the issue, isn't it? "If I get that close to those people, their problems will end up being my problems, and their issues will be my issues, and I will end up smelling just like them." We grow used to our own smell—it doesn't seem so bad. But that guy, that girl—they're just wrong. No one wants to smell like that.

Well, except Jesus.

Scripture doesn't refer to us as individual people so much as it calls us the church. One church, one Lord, one smell. "Look how they love one another and how they care for one another: They've become one with one another."

Introduction

No, this isn't one of those books. I've read those books; I've been to the seminars. In some of them, the author is the pastor of a church of ten thousand members, which he planted three years ago, starting with just his family, in a town of nineteen people. Now he is writing the three (or seven, or twelve) easy steps for you to follow to grow a church just like his. Too many churches, church workers, and good Christian folk have spiritual histories that are strewn with failed attempts at following steps like those, so no, this won't be one of those books.

In others, the author spends a great deal of time finding fault with the current church in America. She will often spend time clearly identifying the many and various issues, while you nod your head in mental agreement because she's right: You see it in your own congregation, in your own people. You feel worse and worse until you get to the end, where you realize that the solutions you thought would be offered aren't there. Now you see the problems more clearly than ever . . . but there seems less hope than ever, too, so no, this won't be one of those books, either.

This book proposes to be an invitation. It is an invitation to come along on a short journey. A journey of failure and celebration. A journey of finding answers and discovering need. A journey of ordinary people following an extraordinary God. It is my prayer that by the time you are done reading you will say to yourself, "This guy is a moron! But look what God is doing anyway!" You would be right if you did. I hope the next thing you think is, "Well, if God will work through him, then maybe He will through me too."

Our ultimate destination is so far away that it's difficult to see, but somewhere in the hazy distance is a city built on a hill, a city whose center—socially, economically and spiritually—is the church. Not my church. Not your church. The Church. The body of Christ working together in koinonia to carry God's light and love into the chaos of smelly people who are dying for the lack of it.

As hazy as the vision is, I would like to encourage you toward that destination. I want to let you, your family, your people and your church know that it is possible. From here, in the center of one American city, I want you to hear that God is still at work through people like you. He is still doing the things that He always did. He hasn't left; He hasn't forgotten. I want to encourage you by showing you some failures, as well as some successes; by telling you some stories about God working in the lives of ordinary people, in an ordinary city, in an ordinary church. Nothing special, nothing amazing from a human perspective, but when God was done, there was something new going on. Something good. Even something very good.

My hope and my prayer is that you're willing to go back out there and try again; that you will come away with a new vision of fresh opportunities. I want you to see and taste and feel it coming. I would like to show you that maybe you're further along than you thought.

And I'd like to celebrate what God has already done. We shouldn't be where we are: a dying urban church that grew; a people that serve; a community that is becoming koinonia. We have smelly people, who in a smelly fashion are willing to get themselves into other people's smelly behavior and make a difference. That's worth a celebration.

But I'd also like to mourn just a little bit, and point out that it's really still a mess. We're not seeing massive growth. Our church hasn't exploded from twelve to twelve hundred in the last three years (more like fifty to two hundred in the first eight. We added another one hundred in the next eight. While there are multiple services, languages and colors we are not, by any stretch, the uber-successful, mega-church from that last conference you attended). We're not seeing community like we want it, and we're not seeing people saved as fast as we'd like. There's still much to do, and we make a lot of mistakes. We are still smelly people, after all.

I guess I'm hoping this will be a smelly kind of book. Are you willing to continue reading? You might want to be careful, or you will risk getting some on you.

1

To Begin With

Death and Failure

$\mathcal{W}$hen I first arrived at Trinity Evangelical Lutheran Church in Cleveland, Ohio, in 1992, the congregation was fairly typical: they were all nice, good-hearted people, their hair color varied (for the most part) from gray to blue, and not one of them knew what to do anymore. Back in 1914, they had had about fourteen hundred members, but they hadn't experienced two consecutive years of growth since. Their last attempt had been the creation of a Spanish-speaking congregation called *El Buen Pastor* that, when combined with Trinity's congregation, added up to around one hundred members. But then there was the fight over who didn't keep the kitchen clean, or whatever it was, and Buen Pastor found another building, rallied the community to raise some funds to remodel it, and before they were done, they had a Spanish-speaking church that was meeting just a block away and Trinity was right back to where it had started. There had been talk since the seventies of closing the church completely, and they were pretty sure I was their last shot.

"So, Pastor Jeff, I guess you go ahead and do whatever you think is best," they said, but most of them had very little real hope.

To be honest, they didn't really have much reason for hope. Statistically speaking, the number of churches that turn around after any length of decline is next to nothing, because (in my experience at least) most churches are unable to admit that they just don't know. Generally speaking, no matter how long or steep their decline, the people in a church will stubbornly cling to the notion that they know what church is supposed to look like, what the pastor is supposed to do, and how it's all supposed to work. Unless either the pastor or the congregation have gone through enough death and failure to know that they don't know, then sooner or later that church will be forced to close their doors. Even when they have, it still sometimes happens.

Fortunately for Trinity, both the congregation and I had been through enough death and failure that we had a shot.

We'll go into detail about my own early failures later on, but I could tell that Trinity had had its fill, because if the congregation had had any life left in them, they never would have put up with me. I tried to tell them early on that I wasn't here to shepherd them and hold their hands, but they didn't believe it until I didn't show up at the hospital the first time one of them got sick, or I wasn't Johnny-on-the-spot for one of the shut-in calls, and such visits got further and further apart instead of closer and closer together. If they'd had any life in them at all, then they'd have gotten rid of me in a minute. I even offered. I said, "Look, if you want a pastor, let's get you one, but I'm a missionary. I'm here to reach the people who are not in our building yet. If you want to work with me to do that, I welcome your support. If you don't, then let's amicably part ways right now."

The people at Trinity were close enough to despair to give me a window. The first thing I did was bust up all the cliques and power structures. And how did I accomplish such a monumental undertaking, you ask? I am honestly not sure. My best guess is that I simply wasn't smart enough to pay any attention to them, and I just went ahead and did whatever I thought needed to be done. By the time they realized that everything was going to be different, there were more new people than there were old people, and the former were outvoting the latter.

Hank Moore, one of the people who was here then, told me that he had often felt like an outsider because he'd arrived later in life, with just his wife and kids, whereas most everybody else was part of extended families who had been here for generations. Everybody sat in their regular seats, and newcomers had to work to gain an inside track. Hank said that, as far as he was concerned, the real work was all done in the first two or three years. Once all the cliques were broken up, and the traditional power structures overturned, anybody could have grown a church.

I guess that I should be either very happy or very sad. Either I did a great a job in those first three years, or I haven't really accomplished much in the last fifteen, but Hank is an honest guy.

The Role of Visionary

*W*ithin a couple months of my arrival at Trinity, I took the church leadership out on a vision retreat. It was August, and we were staying in a fifth-wheel trailer that a member used as a summer cabin. It was by a lake, but there was no air conditioning, and it was hideously hot. I worried we might lose some of the older leaders to heart attacks and strokes, but we soldiered on and spent about twelve hours taking apart the whole church.

I asked them to imagine that there was no Trinity Church on West 30th and Lorain, but that we were going to build one. I asked them to tell me what that church should look like, not architecturally, but as a community. Then we talked about how that ideal matched up against the present reality, and what we could do to bring the two into closer alignment. Basically, "How do we get from where we are now to where we know we're supposed to be?" By the end of that day, we were all hot and miserable. If I hadn't been riding back to Cleveland with somebody else, I think I would have cried, because at the end of those hot, grueling hours, what they'd come up with was that I should probably visit the shut-ins more frequently.

I had assumed, back then, that anybody could "do vision," and it took me six more months to figure out that some people just can't. To me, it was like finding out that some people can't see color; but the conclusion I eventually came to was that this sort of vision is a gift, and the predominant gift of Trinity's leadership at that time was not vision, but problem-solving. I also discovered through the following years that this was fairly typical. After decades of declining membership, the problem-solvers tend to be the only ones left, because every year there were problems to be solved. They would get another budget they couldn't make, and they would have to figure out how to make one. And they succeeded. Problem solved, for now. They didn't necessarily take down the "Bridge Is Out" sign and make a new bridge out of it, but they would make their budget. In the meantime, any former visionaries had wearied of this approach and moved on to greener pastures.

A visionary, it seems to me, is someone who walks into a town meeting and says, "Why isn't there a road through the mountains between here and the city on the other side?" And everyone shrugs their shoulders and says, "We don't know. We've always just gone around." The visionary can see what isn't there, and if he's really passionate, he can build up excitement and enthusiasm for creating it. He is not, on the other hand, the best one to do the actual building. By the time the construction equipment arrives, the visionary is often moving on to the next project. Someone else has to draw up the plans, another has to supervise the work, and still others drive the dump trucks and steam rollers, and maybe the finished product doesn't look exactly the way the visionary envisioned it—maybe it had to curve a little because digging a tunnel wasn't feasible—but the road is completed, and people can now get to the city in half the time. This is the point at which somebody has to sit and collect the tolls to pay for the whole thing. This is often the role many pastors and church leaders find themselves in—sitting in the toll booth for thirty years, collecting coins and making sure the streets are swept and the gutters cleaned. Somebody's got to do that, but it can't be the guy who sees the next road, and it can't be the surveyor, or the construction crew. They'd go crazy being cooped up in a toll booth all day.

The trick is to make sure everybody's doing what they're gifted to do. You don't make the ditch digger design the road, and you don't put the dreamer in the toll booth, because pretty soon he's going to be dreaming up a new way to collect tolls so he doesn't have to sit there all day, and he won't be paying any attention at all to the cars that are blowing by without paying.

Building Hope in the City was, in part, a vision for a road through the mountains. The mountains, in this case, were the many ministries that had erupted at Trinity as people in the congregation started to catch the vision of what the church can be, everything from after-school tutoring to refugee training. At first we had no trouble funding them because most were inexpensive to run. Eventually some of our outside donors started saying, "I don't know if I should keep sending money to Trinity, you know, our church needs new carpeting," or whatever it was they needed, and so I said, "What if we had this separate thing?" and they said, "Oh, I could give money to that. I could give time to that as well. That would be exciting."

Cross-Cultural PR

*A*side from the visionary, the construction workers and the tollbooth sitters, a successful project needs people to hear about it or it won't be successful. Brian Upton, the Assistant Director of Building Hope in the City, had a successful career in marketing before he started attending Trinity, and I'm a natural self-promoter, so between the two of us there was simpatico when it came to public relations. We managed to find new and interesting ways to broadcast to a larger audience, and we did it in a reasonably first-class kind of a way. Nothing looked shoddy, no typical church newsletter material. People could tell that it was better than that, and that made them think that the ministry here was something different, as well. I confess there were times we felt like we were "tricking people for Jesus" or something.

At our city-wide Hymn-Fest at Severance Hall (which is one of the great old-time concert halls in Cleveland), where we'd get about fifteen hundred people to gather and sing these wonderful old-time hymns together, folks would approach me in their black tie and their tails and say things like, "So, this urban work is the real deal, huh?" and I'd get angry. I wanted to scream, "This isn't the part that is real! Fine dining, concert halls and nice clothing do not make what we do real."

But you know what? A cross-cultural guy like me should have known better than that. If you don't speak to people in a language they understand, they're never going to hear you. You can't just ignore that rule because the boundary you're crossing is financial. At least in this regard people are still people no matter what color their skin is or how much green they have.

A lot of the success in the early years had to do with the fact that people in a lot of different parts of the community saw us as real, because we communicated in a way they understood. People sometimes wondered why some of our events didn't have a more "urban" feel to them. My response was, "Look, my target audience for this event isn't the poor, urban community. My target audience might be the upper-middle class suburbanites for that evening, so I bring in groups and music that they like, not the groups and music that I think we should shove down their throats." Then people thought I was pandering. "Well, no, it's just that we're trying to expand our cultural awareness, not theirs. If I get a different group of people that I'm trying to reach, I'll use a different kind of music." We try to decide on worship music, speakers or events, not on what

I like, but based on what the people I'm trying to reach would like. What would best facilitate them hearing the message we have.

Hopefully this book can do the same thing. I knew before I started that there would be scores of people it doesn't reach. If we need to, I will say it again in a different way or I'll have to do another book (or maybe a different medium) for them, but that's okay. I know there are an awful lot of folks out there who are in a similar place to where I was back then. Many of them are pretty sure they're failures. They're pretty sure it's not working, and they are really not sure what to do about it. Many have been at it long enough that they don't think anything is ever going to help. They see the handful of superstars out there with giant churches and national recognition, and they see that it hasn't happened to them yet, and now they're pretty sure that it never will, so they've given up. They have ducked into their version of the toll booth I mentioned earlier and they're going to work out this "little church" thing, and then they're going to retire and hope the retirement holds up. That is not what they wanted, not what they had dreamed of, but it is what they are starting to settle for.

✳ If you're one of those people, I want you to know that you don't have to settle. I want to encourage you to step out of your toll booth and consider building a new road, to reach new people in new ways. Set aside your knowledge of how things are supposed to work and listen to God. He is the author of The Book, not just "a book." He is the one who still calls us to be willing to risk death and failure (at least metaphorically if not actually) in pursuit of what He puts in front of us. ✳

Risky Investments

*G*od is the source of all gifts, and ideally the visionaries, the problem-solvers and everyone else should work together in harmony, but unfortunately, they rarely do. One of the most common sources of tension has to do with the people's attitude toward risk. Problem-solvers are notoriously risk-averse, whereas visionaries tend to thrive on taking leaps of faith.

Not far from Trinity there used to be a German church that was so independent they didn't even belong to a denomination. They had been around since the eighteen hundreds, and they were about ready to fold. They came to me and said, "We see what you're doing, how involved you are in the community, and we would like you to take our building, and to make sure that the work of God continues there after we're gone. If you can promise us that, then we'd be happy to give it to you." I said, "I'd be happy to promise that."

Along with the building came a small but significant sum of money that they still had in the bank, so I was pretty confident I could speak for the church leaders and commit to taking them up on the offer, which just goes to show how little I knew about some of my church leaders at the time. Their answer was "Absolutely not. Buildings are a millstone around our neck as it is," which was true enough, but the buildings we had didn't come with money attached to them. Mostly, they were worried about liability. "What if the roof starts leaking? Then we've got a repair bill on our hands." I said, "Well, yeah, but . . . ," but they wanted nothing to do with it, so Building Hope in the City took it. We ended up all but giving it to a Spanish-speaking Pentecostal church. Even though they ended up paying us next to nothing, we still came out of the whole deal with the original money which was more than we would have had otherwise.

The president of the church came to us after the sale and asked if Trinity would see any of that money. "Well, no. Building Hope assumed all the risk you were so worried about."

The same thing happened in another congregation when the opportunity arose to get a free intern for a year. Again, leadership brought up the question of liability. "What if the intern has a medical emergency? Then we'll feel responsible for taking care of it." So, once again, Building Hope in the City decided it was worth the risk and took the intern. We took on the intern, she got some amazing work done in the community, and when she moved on to do church work in Iowa, she ended up sending us groups of twenty or twenty-five people every summer to continue serving in Cleveland, get the same training from us that she got and multiplying the investment we made over and over again.

Opportunities like this come to us all the time, and by "us," I don't just mean Trinity or Building Hope in the City. They come to each of us as individuals, too. If you're passionately pursuing God, and He puts something in front of you, you recognize it for what it is. Otherwise, you see it as a liability waiting to hang you. If your question isn't, "How can we make this work?" but instead you ask, "How will this end up working us?" then you're going to turn down a lot of those opportunities. I know liabilities need to be considered, but taking the children into the desert was a huge and smelly liability as well. It was still the wisest course of action.

Often those opportunities are going to be people. And a lot of those people won't be coming out of nice, clean backgrounds. In fact, they're going to end up taking a lot of your time and energy. They might not do things the way you'd like them to be done, and maybe they're not always on the same page as you, but you can either see them as a liability and say, "No, thank you; I need somebody who knows how to organize better than that," or, you can see them as gifts from God and figure your way through the chaos.

If there's one thing I hope this book should demonstrate clearly, it's that there is no end to the chaos and the smell that comes with it. I'm not sure you ever should organize or grow your way out of it.

2

Move Forward

Hiding in the Church

I'm hiding in the church again. Sometimes I go to the garage or the attic, and sometimes to a coffee shop, but today it's the sanctuary. I wanted to get some writing done, but in the office the phones are still ringing, and the doorbell is still dinging, so now I'm sitting in a pew. Funny that no one will think to look for the pastor in the church.

This morning I have had a gas shut-off for a family with a young child, followed by a woman running from an abusive husband. Close on her heels was a lady who is on her way back from a hearing in which she found out that she has lost her food stamp privileges. Our Internet went out and all access was lost. In the conversation with a very nice man from the phone company whose Indian accent was very thick, I was interrupted by an argument between two of our volunteers in the food pantry. Something about somebody's children, and somebody else's niece said something to someone, and . . . I admit it: I checked out and went to hide in the church.

The prophet Isaiah, in the twenty-fourth chapter says:

The city of confusion is broken down;
Every house is shut up, so that none may go in.
There is a cry for wine in the streets,
All joy is darkened,
The mirth of the land is gone.
In the city, desolation is left,
And the gate is stricken with destruction.

For a moment there I thought he was talking about my neighborhood. With words like confusion, desolation, stricken, destruction . . . Sheesh—he might be talking about my life.

Dirt and chaos. It seems like it's everywhere. You could try to control it, corral it, get a handle on it. Put it all into neat piles—columns and rows—the line forms in the back and please take a number. Applying order to your world may seem to be holding the dirt at bay, but if you look carefully, there are probably some cracks around the edges where it keeps oozing in no matter how hard you try.

You could try hiding, like me, but hiding won't last. The chaos will find you eventually. Some people hide behind anger or money. Some use secretaries and locks on their doors. We have entire housing complexes devoted to fences, gates and guards along with rules governing behavior, all in an effort to keep the madness, the chaos and the dirtiness of the world away. In the last extreme, some even sink into a personal world of madness and chaos which protects them for awhile. But not even that will last forever.

More and more my heroes in life are the people who embrace the mess. They root around in the filth and accept the chaos and take joy in passionately following God into the lives of messy people.

Pastor Matt's Tank Theory

*W*hen Pastor Matt Williams was in fifth grade, his daddy moved their family across town to the "right" side of the tracks. Years later, Matt would point to that move as a deciding factor in his decision, not just to be a pastor, but to enter into ministry among the poor. On the poor side of the tracks, Matthew had had plenty of friends. On the wealthier side of the tracks, he sat alone at the swing-set and made friends slowly in the classroom. On the poor side of town, Matt had hung out with kids who didn't look like him, but who liked him. African-American kids, Hispanic kids, and white kids spent time playing together, making fun of each other, even hurting each other, but everybody knew who was who and what was what. Here on the new side of town almost everybody looked like him, but nobody seemed to like him. Thus, he learned at an early age that having the same skin color did not necessarily make you the same, and that being different wasn't bad. His desire to go back to the poor side of the tracks caused him, in his adult life, to choose to work in urban ministry among similar low-income neighborhoods filled with African-American, Latino and white folks. You find them all in the neighborhood around Mt. Calvary Church on Cleveland's West Side.

Mt. Calvary had been declining for many years and showed all of the signs of an imminent death, but Pastor Williams was excited. There were poor people of all different colors in the neighborhood. Lots of opportunities to do the thing that he knew he was called to do: Preach the gospel to the lost and heal the broken. Pastor Williams went to work (sometimes alongside the church, sometimes in opposition to them), and when money grew tight he took a job at the high school teaching religion and encouraging, counseling, and challenging students and faculty alike. He took great joy in both his jobs, but there was always more to do and never enough money to go around. Once, after a particularly grueling day, I asked him how he managed to keep going, and he told me he'd been a tank driver in the army. He went on to explain that there are three basic rules to driving a tank:

Once you're in, you're in.

The only pedal is for go.

You can change direction, but you can't really steer.

Tanks were first introduced by the British during World War I as a means to break the deadlock of trench warfare, but in order to conceal their true purpose they were designated as vehicles capable of carrying large quantities of water. These "water tanks" were not built for comfort, so getting into a tank is not the easiest task, and Matt was not a small man. All the levers, handles and controls are necessary, but they make for cramped space. And when I say that Matt was no small son of the South, I mean, he was ample in girth. For this reason, according to brother Williams, the idea of jumping out is not part of the mind-set. You and the tank are going into battle as a unit, and chances are, if the tank doesn't make it through the battle, then neither do you. Although saying so could make him sound like a two hundred and fifty pound Yoda with a southern accent, a phrase he used frequently was, "With the tank, become one, you must."

He felt the same way about his life. "God has put me in this place for a purpose. He has me in this church and this community for his purpose," he would say. "No sense asking why or for how long. We have a battle to fight and a war to win. Once you're in, you're in."

Now, I have never driven a tank, so I have to take his word for it, but according to Matt, there is only one pedal, and it's for go. The only question is, "Are you going to use it?"

Backing up was never really in Pastor Matt's vocabulary. Once a direction or a purpose was established for his life, his church, or his neighborhood, then "go" was the operative word. If it was the right thing to do, then now was the time to do it. No hesitations, no more discussing, just go.

There are mechanisms in a tank that are for braking the individual tracks, which allows the driver to turn to the right or the left, but, according to Matt, it's more of a controlled chaos than it is steering. Generally speaking, you point your tank in an appropriate direction and hope for the best. While this tendency sometimes frightened the more timid people around him, it was a part of who he was.

All of this may have included some exaggeration in order to make a point (he was always capable of that), but his three rules of tank-driving fit my experience in the city as well. Each day I wake up believing I know where the day is going. Each day I am proven wrong. Passion is required to continue forward without a clear map and committing myself to what God has put in front of me saves me a lot of time asking why questions. Whether the topic is marriage, church, job, neighborhood, or ministry, being able and willing to unhesitatingly accept reality helps clear out the distractions that, as the author of Hebrews puts it, "so easily entangle us" (12:1).

Pastor Matt Williams was an amazing guy. In him I saw passion for the Lord and His work being lived out every day. The Lord of Hosts called him home not too long ago. I lost a friend, a neighbor, and a fellow soldier who wasn't yet forty years old. I wanted to ask why. I wanted to change course. But I have the same orders as Brother Williams had, and the same commanding officer. So, for today, I am in. Passionately in. And I am staying in. With that decided, it is time to use the only pedal I am given and go. I will do my best to keep us heading in the right direction, but in the apparent chaos around me, I will leave the steering to God.

Seeing Through the Chaos

Ours is not the first generation to deal with chaos so thick you need a tank to get through it. Back in the early nineteen hundred's, when Pastor Pieper (whose grandfather wrote the dogmatics texts that many Lutherans have to study in seminaries today) was the pastor at Trinity, he went out into the street one day to break up a brawl between a couple of drunken German congregants, got knocked to the curb, hit his head and died. Very soon afterwards (because this was a big, important church at the time, and they needed a pastor), his family was moved out of the parsonage. No dad, no job, no home. The eldest boy went to work, provided a home and an income, so that the rest of the kids in the family could go to college and move elsewhere and do better for themselves. His wife, Peggy, continued to be a member of the congregation until she just recently died.

The story of Pastor Pieper reminds me that there are no guarantees about how this journey through the chaos is going to work out.

The people here in the city don't need any reminders. They're used to pastors arriving, full of passion and zeal, and then leaving, burned out and defeated. Until you've stuck around for six or seven years, they don't mind getting out of you what they can and throwing the neighborhood chaos in your face. In fact, they're proud of the chaos. They love taking you around and watching you go, "Ooooh, my God," when you're introduced to the weirdest freak or most destitute wretch the community has to offer. If you're used to a more middle-class environment, where people often keep their problems to themselves unless it's absolutely necessary (and even then they only share in private), it can be shocking to have somebody tell you, in the midst of a crowded church building, that their mother has been bringing home men or something equally as extreme. You look around and say, "Should everybody really know about this?" and they say, "Oh, pastor, everybody knows about my Mom. She's a whore, and she always has been."

That sort of thing happens over and over until you get numb, and you have to make a choice: You can take the next train out of town, isolate yourself from the pain or you start developing emergency-room syndrome, where you disconnect emotionally from the hurt and heartache and tragedy enough to allow you to stay and help as best as you're able. There isn't really another option, because the barrage is constant.

A lot of the houses around here have ten, fifteen people at a time living in them, and it's hard to tell who's related to whom. Someone will stop calling her biological mother "Mom," and go live with this other woman who treats her like a mom should, and she'll start to call this woman "Mom." In the meantime, none of her brothers and sisters are talking to her because of how she treated their mom, but they're also calling all these other women "sister." I feel bad for social workers and others who legally need to know, but as a pastor, the line you have to walk inside the chaos gets really fine. Being in such close proximity with each other leads to all kinds of illicit and immoral things, and there you are in the middle of it. Many people are used to a family being a family, and if you're my mom, I call you "Mom," and if you're not my mom, I don't. Cousins are cousins, brothers are brothers and if we're not related then I'll call you my friend. But that's not the way it always works down here. Relational chaos is one way that formally black and white lines seem to blur and even break, and as a representative of God you are left to ask good missionary questions.

Culture is a label we use to sum up the distinctive characteristics of a way of life for a particular people. As a country we have multiple cultures and sub-cultures that must be navigated, sometimes simultaneously. Our legal culture is different than what we celebrate in pop culture. Everyone seems to see a difference between the culture of our "fly-over" states and our coastal cities. The real color, in my mind, that separates us is not black, white and brown but green. The cultural differences between the poor and the middle-class can be canyon in size.

You find many of these cultures here in the city and it is that mixing together that brings us chaos. Some of the things you witness should get turned in, legally, but the moment I report one thing to the authorities, I'm no longer pastoring down here in the neighborhood—I am perceived as working for the system instead. You can stand up at the front of the church and talk to the nice people with cleaned up lives all you want, but you won't be going back into the chaos anymore, because you can't be trusted.

I mean if it's something really horrible and everybody's standing around saying, "Yeah, somebody should do something," then you do something, but you do it yourself. You don't call the police on your neighbors because their dogs are loud; you go next door to talk to your neighbors because their dogs are loud. When they're screaming at their children should you call the cops and turn them in or do you go next door and talk to them about it? Unfortunately, the second approach may lead to you getting thrown out of the house, and now they're still screaming at their children, but you don't have access anymore. Ah, but if you call the cops now, then everybody knows who called them, because you were the one over there, so there goes any hope for anonymity.

Our society has set up boundary lines to protect us from the chaos, but they were set up by a middle-class system, and they're understood by middle—and upper-middle-class kinds of people. The people down here don't always get them, and they don't fit well with who we are and what we're doing, so if you can't persevere through the chaos without using the system against your own people, you won't get very far.

Certainly you can and should be calling from the pulpit for dads to be better fathers, speaking out against drug and alcohol abuse, and addressing domestic violence as part of your conversation with the community, but you have to live in the chaos all the same. You begin to get a glimpse of the enormity of the incarnation and what John was trying to communicate when he wrote "the Word became flesh and dwelt among us" (John 1:14).

My task, as I see it, is to stand up in the crow's nest, look through the chaos and sight land for the community and then cheer them onward. I spent a lot of time, in the early days, trumpeting all of Trinity's successes, and very little talking about all the failures. Any time I ever went out of town, I would come back and thank them for being the best church on the planet. I would highlight where the church I just went to had all of these flawed ways of thinking, and congratulate them on not being or believe any of that. I was reinforcing what I wanted them to have, and hoping they'd believe it if they heard it often enough. Well, you know God was good and at some point they started saying, "Wait a minute. That's not who we are, this is who we are," and it started to work.

When I first began at Trinity, I announced, back in 1992, that we were going to have two hundred members by the year 2000, they said, "Pastor, have you looked around here? Who are you going to reach? Even if you get two hundred people, they couldn't pay the bills on this place." And they were right about that, but, sometimes, when you're trying to see through the chaos, you can't let yourself get too mired in reality. You've got to see above and beyond it, outside of it, and to see the Spirit of the Lord hovering over the waters, and believe that He's about to do something, that He's about to act. Our call is to get on board with that, whatever it is, and go forward, because He's not going to leave it to "*to hu wabohu*" forever. We will talk about the phrase to hu wabohu later, but for now let's just call it chaos.

When the first Spanish-speaking family started coming, they fit right in. They were this huge extended family of maybe twenty people. Mothers, brothers, sisters, cousins, all of them arrived together, and I went, "Woooooohoooooooo! We've got sixty people in church!" The trouble was, if a husband and wife among them was having a fight and weren't going to church, then nobody else wanted to show up, either, and I'd think, "Booooohoooooo!" Except publicly all I'd say was, "Yay for us!" (and then just not say a whole lot about the week we were back to forty). And the week after that, when they all came back, I'd say, "Yay for us!" again.

My job was to find a way through the chaos, but it was never to find a way out of it, because the people identified with the chaos so strongly that they didn't want to leave it behind. A little purpose to it, a little focus, would be fine, but they didn't want to become suburban or anything horrible like that. A little hope would be nice. "You know, maybe I don't want my kids to go to college. Maybe I want them to stay right here with me, but it would be great if they could all get jobs, and we could buy up all the houses on this street as they become available, and this could be our little street. And maybe that doesn't seem like much of a dream to you, but if you could show me a way through the chaos to that, I could get behind you."

When I first got into the neighborhood, I had a fight out in front of the office with a guy named Fred who's still around, and still homeless. Fred will be just fine for a few days. His people skills aren't necessarily great; he'll tell bad jokes to the wrong people, and he'll come up with the same stuff all the time, but in the end, he's a good guy. He's here early, he stays late and he does what he can to help out. But you can tell when his mental state is starting to waver, because he starts to get angry. He'll go off into a corner mumbling to himself, and pretty soon he's calling out every black person in the place because they're driving our country down into the toilet, or he's threatening to go after every foreigner he can find because it's all their fault. He'll start a rant like that, and it won't be forty-five minutes before I'll have him off the property and gone, and he won't be around again for another six or eight weeks. It was during one of those rants that he grabbed me, and started wrestling with me out on the front porch of the office.

Well, nothing much came of it, I mean, he knocked my glasses off, and when he saw them on the ground, he stepped on them before running away, but that was it. But it was pretty symbolic of a lot of what went on in those early years. It wasn't really fighting. It was more like wrestling for no apparent purpose. Yeah, it cost me, and yeah, I wish it wouldn't have happened, but that's what you've got down here. So, what am I going to do? I could hide out in the church, being all visionary while other people handle the walk-ins, maybe call the police when Fred stirs up trouble, or I could get actively, physically involved, and risk getting my glasses stepped on, or worse, because my vision for the church is bigger than Sunday morning and maybe a few outreach programs during the week. It's about church being the center of the community, becoming incarnate. If that means that sometimes the chaos in the community becomes chaos in the church, then so be it. The guy in the crow's nest probably needs a new pair of glasses every once in a while.

3

Through the Chaos

Passionate Leaders

While there are many other characteristics that a man or a woman can have that equip them for work among the smelly people of the world, passion is what carries them to the front. Without it, the disciple never travels far enough down the difficult roads. Without it, vision is shortened, and people seldom see the new (though risky) path.

The word *passion* comes from a Latin verb meaning "to suffer" or "to endure." From this verb we retain the idea of intensity, but we now apply this intensity in the positive. "Intense emotion, compelling feeling, enthusiasm, or desire for something. A lively or eager interest in or admiration for a proposal, cause, or activity. Love."

So, from suffering through endurance we arrive at intense emotion and even love. I am not sure that those connections are ever separated. True passion requires suffering and endurance. You can, on the other hand, find endurance without the passion. How many churches have I visited that continue to suffer, and even endure, but they do it in a passionless existence that attracts no one and repels most? How many pastors, moments into a conversation, reveal themselves simply to be doing a job or following a career path? Passion is nowhere to be found, and so the truth of scripture they speak falls flat in their listeners' ears.

I'm not talking about people who are merely outspoken or charismatic. Passionate people may or may not be either. They are often quiet, honest, loyal and self-controlled. Their passion isn't on the surface, but if you dig down just a little you will find it in them.

I would be the first to admit that passion has its disadvantages. I advise college students to consider this carefully before they start writing a paper about a topic they are passionate about. You will put in far more time and effort and the pay-off (grade) is rarely any higher than if you just do the assignment.

Passion will cost you more than if you operate without it. You will spend more time, resources and energy than a less passionate soul would. Passion untempered can lead one down some very wrong paths, and passion without wisdom can damage, hurt, and harm you and the people around you. Passion can be as destructive as it can be creative. Perhaps even more so. You know how I know?

My Testimony

Like Pastor Matt, I was young when my life began to turn for the worse, but it really wasn't because of what someone else did. I was living in Minneapolis and instead of going to school, four or five of my friends and I would all skip. We'd hang out in somebody's garage and pour out canisters from the shelves into little baby food jars. We didn't check to see what they were—as long as it had fumes it would do the job. We'd lean over the baby food jar and breathe in. Every once in awhile I'd sit up, look around and say, "Whooooaaaa." It would wear off pretty quickly, so I'd go back down, and pretty soon the day would be over.

Of course, pot and alcohol were involved as well. The morning after my dad would have a poker party, I'd get up early and run around the house drinking whatever leftover alcohol I could find. I'd usually get a mouthful of cigarette butts in one bottle or another, but that was a price I was willing to pay. Pot was easy to get a hold of back in the sixties and early seventies—everyone was smoking it—but once I was old enough, alcohol became my preferred drug of choice, because, by then, it was the easiest to obtain, and you'd keep yourself out of more trouble if it was alcohol in your system when they arrested you and not some controlled substance. Not that I didn't do those as well, but, as anybody who's been in recovery will tell you, the problem wasn't with the pot or alcohol or acid or crack or coke or any of the stuff that I did through the years, the real issue was me.

Eventually, it reached a point where I tried to run away. I chose the option of going into the military in order to escape myself. It was dumb, because geographic changes never work, but I did it anyway. It was in the Navy that I had my first blackout.

I'd been to a party the night before, and I couldn't find the car anyplace. It was a community vehicle that three or four of us used. I was asking, "Where's the car?" and everybody said, "You should know; you're the one who drove it home." I didn't know what they were talking about. I said, "No, I passed out at the party," and they said, "No, you were driving when you left the place." When I finally found the car, there was a dent on the fender and blood in the dent. To this day I don't know if it was animal or human blood. That scared me badly enough that I didn't have anything to drink for a couple of days, but an even greater fear was that the police would show up looking for me. Well, they never did, and the blackouts started to seem pretty normal after awhile. It reached the point where I would lose twenty-four to thirty-six hours at a time. I'd come around, and I'd stagger back—I wouldn't even know what day it was—and they'd put me in the brig for unauthorized absence. I couldn't tell them what I'd been doing, because I didn't know, but that didn't seem all that strange to me. Certainly I wasn't the only one I knew who had blackouts.

I got busted a couple of times on possession charges when I was stationed in Scotland, where I was working on navigation computers for nuclear missile submarines. Then I got a couple of violations having to do with violent behavior on shore leave. Finally, the shore patrol dragged me off again. I went to a captain's mast and the captain, seeing the progression of charges, decided to offer me another choice: I could serve time in prison, or I could go to rehab. Seemed like a no-brainer to me: Suddenly, rehab sounded like a good idea.

First they sent me to an asylum in Germany, because they thought perhaps I had some mental health issues. I probably did have some mental health issues, coming off the drugs and the alcohol, but what they did there was strap me to a bed facing the ceiling and leave the lights on all night so they could see me. I guess they were afraid I'd hurt myself, but I was only there a day or two before they determined I wasn't a danger to myself; I was just a druggie and a drunk. So they sent me back to a treatment center in Northern Scotland, where it was determined that I needed more help than they were capable of giving. They relocated me to a treatment center in the Great Lakes Service Center in Chicago.

I was caught sleeping with a woman who was also in treatment at the same time. Fraternizing, of course, was strictly prohibited. Also, if I remember correctly, she was related to a guy that was higher up the chain of command than I should have been messing with. We both got thrown out, and, I don't know if it was in retaliation or just the way things went, but I ended up assigned to an aircraft carrier somewhere in the middle of nowhere. Consequences not being high on the list of things I thought about, I took an unauthorized absence. Not AWOL—you have to be gone thrity days before it's actually AWOL—I just stayed gone for twenty-nine days and twenty-three hours. I knew when I returned that the ship would be long gone, and that I would do brig time, but by the time I got out of the brig I'd get new orders to something else that would probably be better than that aircraft carrier. So I got a job for twenty-nine days, earning money under the table, and during that time I cleared my head enough that, by the time I came back, I said, "This is wrong. I shouldn't be doing it this way. I've come back to be a good sailor and clean things up, do my time, and then get out."

I should have known, when you scream for three years to get out, they keep you in, but when you say, "I want in," they throw you out. So they drummed me out at another captain's mast.

Soon after that I got thrown out of Chicago—sort of. I was in a hotel room with four or five other people, and my pockets were full of all kinds of stuff when the police showed up. I was taking off my socks when they arrested us, and pills were falling out of my socks. I didn't even know what I was doing anymore, just had handfuls of Christmas candy—reds and greens and blues and pretty colors. But for whatever reason, one of the officers got me out of the cell in the middle of the night (it seemed like the middle of the night, but then everything was kind of dark and hazy back then), and put me on a bus and said, "Don't come back to Chicago, because the next time you do you're going away for a long time."

He'd gotten my home address off of my civilian driver's license, and I think he must have paid for the bus ticket out of his own pocket. Somehow he arranged for a highway patrolman to meet the bus in Wisconsin, when it stopped for breakfast, just to make sure I got back on the bus. The patrolman bought breakfast even, because I didn't have any money. (Let me take a moment to thank the "men in blue." I had spent years verbally degrading them, consider this a small, though inadequate, payback in print). I got back on the bus and continued on to Minneapolis, where my parents still lived.

I tried to find a job there, but the only work I was really fit for outside the military was construction, and it was the middle of summer—all the college and even high school kids already had taken all of the jobs. I knew how to dig ditches and look like a rube, but everyone else did, too. And then a former employer told me, through my dad, about a job opening they had in Boulder, Colorado. I didn't know anybody in Boulder, but it didn't matter—it was work; it was money. I moved to Boulder. I started out living in the job trailer. It took me months to actually save up enough to get an apartment, inside of which I had a mattress that I rescued from a dumpster, a clock radio that had an alarm on it, a phone and a few pots, pans, and spoons that I borrowed from the lady down the hall who felt sorry for me. I honestly don't remember if I ever gave them back.

I'm no stranger to chaos.

The military had not been kind to me, but they had been honest in their assessment: "You need to get yourself together." But life didn't really change for me when I arrived in Boulder. The scenery was different, there were new people around, but my old patterns and habits were the same. I was still killing myself slowly, with drugs, alcohol, and bad decisions. Despite every opportunity to understand how badly I needed to quit, how badly I needed to change, they were the coping mechanisms I had, the ones I could rely on, at least for temporary relief. And so I drank and I used, I used and I drank.

Then one morning, in October, a morning much like many other mornings, I woke up not feeling really great, so I went for a walk, through the quiet neighborhoods of Boulder, trying to shake off my hangover while I waited for the stores to start selling real beer instead of the three-two variety. I was walking past an older stone church when a voice inside my head reminded me that it been a long time since I had attended a service.

I began to argue. I can't go inside a church, I told myself. I stink. I look bad. Maybe I could go home, get a drink and a shower, and then go to church.

You won't make it back out of the house, a voice in my head told me. You'll never make it to church, if you do that.

"Well, it's too late to go into that one," I told myself. At least, I thought it was me I was talking to. *"I'll go into the next church I walk by."*

Deal.

I don't know how it happened. I was walking along with my head down, trying to make it back to the apartment without passing (or at least noticing) any more churches, but pretty soon I came to one that was almost a block long (including the school building attached to it). Somehow I managed to make it past all of that building before noticing it was there. When I did, I stopped: I was standing at the bottom of the sidewalk that led up to the front doors of the sanctuary.

Okay, fine. I'll go in, but they're going to throw me right back out. They're not going to welcome some smelly guy like me into their nice, clean church.

I went in. They smiled. They brought me over to sign the guest register. Here's a hint—don't sign the guest register unless you want them to come visit you. A little old lady helped with the hymnal and the bulletin. She showed me what to sing and when to sing it.

Somehow I had ended up in a Lutheran church, but I was too embarrassed to tell her that I could sing their liturgies without looking in the book. After the service, they put me in the youth Bible study. I guess even though I was in my mid-twenties, "youth" was the closest study they had. The other one was filled with people over sixty. There were only four people in this teenage Bible study, and now there was me, but I went home that day glad that I had listened and walked in.

Nevertheless, I didn't expect to be back the next week, so when a man from church named Kurt Genslinger started knocking on my door and calling my phone, I stopped answering the door and the telephone, just so I wouldn't have to talk to him.

That December, my company needed a pickup truck driven to North Dakota. "Drive the truck up there and drop it off at the job site," they said, "and if you want to stop in Minnesota to see your family, feel free—just make sure you're back here for work on Monday morning."

What a great opportunity. I loaded my pockets full of black beauties—speed to keep me going—and the truck compartment with miscellaneous reds and greens—Christmas candy—and got ready for a weekend of partying. I drove like a maniac. I think I was going one hundred and twenty in that pickup truck when the hood popped. I thought it was going to come right through the windshield at me. That scared me to death, of course, but it didn't slow me down. Every minute I spent on the road was another minute that I wasn't partying with my friends back home.

You see, I wasn't all that focused on seeing my family; I was going back to see the crew. Except that, when I finally arrived, I couldn't find any of them. I hadn't called ahead or anything, and I had never been good at keeping in touch, but I just assumed they'd be available. I asked around, and one by one I found them. A few were in jail cells. A few more were under grave markers. The others weren't doing so well, either, though they seemed to think that "out of jail" and "above ground" wasn't all that bad.

So I was wandering around Minneapolis, and I began to think—it took me awhile, I'm a little slow—I began to think, "Maybe *there's something wrong with this approach to life."* Even with all the rehab I'd had, I still wasn't sure, but something wasn't working.

I returned to Boulder without quite figuring it out. I went back to work, but found myself struggling with my purpose and direction. Finally, in January, something happened. I can't tell you the day, let alone the hour or the minute when it changed for me. I can't tell you about a shining light or a voice speaking out of the darkness. All I can tell you is that in December all I wanted to do was party a little harder than I'd ever partied before, and by February, all I really cared about was Jesus.

The drugs went pretty quickly. I quit the alcohol, too, for the most part, but from time to time I'd take off my "Jesus is Lord" belt buckle and my "Jesus Christ, King of the Universe" hatpin, sneak off to some bar where no one would know me, and get toasted.

I'd wake up the next morning feeling horrible. Not just from the hangover—I'd feel horrible because I knew I'd let God down.

Up until then, I had forgotten about Kurt and the people at that Lutheran church, but finally I started going back, started participating, speaking out about things that seemed obvious to me. I'm sure most of those people shook their heads privately and wondered if I would ever mature into a full-blown disciple, but I was excited. I was passionate and I needed more.

Six months later, in August, my last drink was behind me, and I had found something in the Bible that I didn't understand. I don't remember what it was; I just remember I needed badly to know what it was God was saying there. I thought of Kurt. He was the Director of Christian Education, and he seemed to have a lot of answers, so I called him up. He didn't answer his phone, so I went to visit him. The buzzer at the front door of his apartment didn't seem to be working, so I thought about all the times I hadn't answered the phone or responded to the doorbell, and I thought, *"He's probably just up there watching TV."*

I looked at the balconies. They were stacked in such a way that, with a little effort, a little risk, I could reach Kurt's sliding glass door on the third floor. I figured I'd knock, he'd let me in, we'd have a laugh, and then he'd tell me the answer to whatever my pressing question was. Well, I clambered up, rail to balcony, rail to balcony, but he didn't answer my knock either, and there was a curtain blocking my view of the inside, so I tried the door. It was unlocked. I slid the door open and stepped inside.

"Kurt? Kurt?"

I found him in his bedroom, fast asleep. I don't know what he had done wrong for God to put him through something like that, but I scared him to death. He was yelling and screaming, while I was saying, "Kurt, I just have this one little question about Scripture." I had left off pursuing the ultimate high, and now I was pursuing God, just as passionately, and just as chaotically. God bless him, once Kurt got over his fright, he even did his best to answer my question.

Some months later, he and I and another guy moved into a house together, and I found out that, yeah, he just goes to bed early. At the time, I couldn't imagine why anyone would go to bed at that time of night. I don't care if you're not using anymore, going to bed that early just seemed crazy.

Anyway, that passion led me to all kinds of strange behavior, because, man, if it's in there, and that made God happy, then that's what I wanted to do. If I could have found a Cannanite, I'm sure I would have thought about killing him, and certainly would have never let my daughter marry him. I got involved in all kinds of stuff that were maybe on the fringe of Christian practice, but I didn't know any better: I was passionately interested in doing what God wanted. That's all that mattered.

So what matters most to you? When you woke up today, was He on your mind? Couldn't wait to get your day started to see what He had for you? Searched the scripture waiting for a word—any word—from Him for you?

Nah, me neither.

Let's pray.

Lord Jesus, help us to passionately follow you today. Send your Holy Spirit and fill us with your passion for the world. Stir in us an uneasiness to accept anything less than you. Oh, and Lord, a little wisdom might be a good idea as well. In Jesus' name. Amen.

Aliza's Dog

*A*liza has a dog. His name is Rocco. She and the dog both love to go the beach. Rocco loves to run on the shore, Aliza loves hunting for shells, and they both enjoy the sun, the sand, and the water. There is, however, a significant difference between them when it comes to dead fish. Aliza tries to avoid them at all cost. Fish that washed up on shore hours or days before stink up the whole area and steal some of her enjoyment. The beach no longer seems as pure or wholesome.

Rocco, on the other hand, seems to consider dead fish a feast for the senses. Something about dead, rotting fish draws him. He will sniff them for a moment, nudge them with his nose and then . . . he rolls. Not just over them but *in* them. Rolls and squirms as if he can't get enough of the stink. Soon his back, sides, ears . . . everything is covered in rotting fish, and Rocco is grinning from ear to ear.

Why does he do it? Why would he purposely coat himself in the thing that his master so dislikes? "Bad dog" isn't enough to stop him. Nothing short of a leash will keep him away from the chum.

Do you sometimes wonder: "Why do people do the things they do?" Here's a better question: "Why do *I* do some of the things I do?"

Why did I eat that last piece of cake? Why did I blow up at my son like that? Why can't I be positive and cheerful all the time? Why do I let things get me down? Am I describing anyone you know? I mean, besides me?

The struggle between clean and dirty is no small battle. Then again, neither is the struggle between darkness and light. Before we knew God, we ran, we turned our backs on Him and His call to be cleansed. In our running we subjected ourselves to untold hardship and pain. God, as He did in the first chapter of Isaiah asks, "Why should you be stricken again?" Still, we run, we struggle, and we shake our fist. *Leave us in our filth. We like it this way. This is the life we have chosen.* Calling for us to be cleansed, God pursues us as we struggle.

Some of us were compelled. "We came to believe," as it says in the twelve-step program, "that a power greater than ourselves could restore us to sanity." The struggle appears to be over. The endurance has turned to love for the one who cleansed us. Once washed in the waters of baptism and cleansed from our sin before God, however, a strange thing happens. God now calls us to get dirty again. Often, when he does, we begin again our resistant ways. We still don't seem to mind the dirt we are familiar with, but other people's filth—ugh. We have some passion for our Lord, but for people of a different smell, well, not so much.

In Colossians, Chapter 1, Paul writes from prison to the new church and talks about his hopes, his passion and his prayer for them:

> "For this cause we also, since the day we heard it, do not cease to pray for you, and to desire that you might be filled with the knowledge of His will in all wisdom and spiritual understanding; That you might walk worthy of the Lord unto all pleasing, being fruitful in every good work, and increasing in the knowledge of God; Strengthened with all might, according to His glorious power, unto all patience and long suffering with joyfulness; Giving thanks unto the Father, which hath made us meet to be partakers of the inheritance of the saints in light." (Colossians 1:9-12).

It is worth noting, first, what he does not pray for. With all of the violence of the ancient world at that time he does not pray that they would have peace. Though many, if not most, of the Colossian Christians are poor, he does not pray for prosperity, in the financial sense of the word. No mention here of physical health, family, or any of the things that we so often pray for on behalf of others. I am not saying that Paul never prayed for these things, but if he did, we have no record of it.

He prayed in a very specific way. "We pray . . . that you might be filled with the knowledge of His will in all wisdom and spiritual understanding." Paul and his companions are praying for the Colossians to have the kind of knowledge that would get them dirty.

I love the idea that the guards chained to Paul had to listen in while he and others (we hope) prayed for this specific, full and complete knowledge that would bring eternal salvation. How many guards were saved because they were chained to such prayers?

> "For though I am absent in the flesh, yet am I with you in the spirit, joying and beholding your order, and the steadfastness of your faith in Christ. As ye have therefore received Christ Jesus the Lord, so walk ye in Him: Rooted and built up in Him, and established in the faith, as ye have been taught, abounding therein with thanksgiving." (Colossians 2:5-7).

Apparently, going out there to get dirty is not enough for the apostle. His prayer for these people of Colossae is that it continues. He prays that this full knowledge of God leads them into the messy lives of those around them. He prays that they would become so used to this form of dirt, this chaos, that they would start to take nourishment there. He prays that they would put down roots. His desire is that they would begin to draw strength from it all because that is where they will find the vine, the Christ.

That they would be rooted "in Christ" doesn't sound odd to our ears. He is the vine and we know that being connected to Him is mandatory for our survival. The disciples seemed to be vaguely familiar with this idea as well. Peter said, "To whom should we go? You have the words of eternal life."

Rooted in Christ is where we want to be, but He seems to stay rooted in the dirt of life. Staying connected to Him means being close to it, as well, and Paul appears to understand that. He writes, after all, from prison. His list is famous: shipwrecks, stonings, beatings, and persecution. Of course he follows a Lord who was himself killed as He loved his people and so he can say to anyone else who would hear it, "Follow me as I follow Christ," and, "Join me in suffering for the gospel." It is this life in which he encourages us to walk and in this Christ that he asks us to take root.

And yet, we are not called to contribute to the dirt and chaos, but to shed the light and holiness of Christ into those dark places. The problem is that we inevitably get more *on* us than rubs off *from* us.

St. Paul was a man of intellect and insight. He was impassioned and inspired, disciplined and devout, sensitive and sincere. And yet, for all that, St. Paul could write, "I can will what is right, but I cannot do it. For I do not do the good I want, but the evil I do not want is what I do." (Romans 7:18-19).

I confess that I am like Paul . . . and Rocco. It seems I can hardly wait for some festering, rotting, sinful behavior to appear before I am rolling around in it and covered from ears to tail. Trapped by my own desires, my own need, I am again where I said I would never again be.

St. Paul, in Chapter 7 of Romans, describes for us the war going on in his own mind and body. He describes himself as a wretched man, and he cries out, "Who will deliver me?" And then, in verse 25, he answers his own question: "Thanks be to God—through Jesus Christ our Lord!" Jesus Christ delivered him, just as Christ can deliver you and me.

While there are many other characteristics that a man or a woman can have that equip them for work among the smelly people of the world, passion is what carries them to the front. Without it, the disciple never travels far enough down the difficult roads. Without it, vision is shortened, and people seldom see the new (though risky) path. Still, passion can easily turn the wrong direction, and all things followed passionately are not, necessarily the right things.

There is little else to be said when it comes to passion and sin. Left to myself, I stink. I become passionate in all the wrong directions while I pursue folly. Someone will have to take me home and give me a bath. Funny, when He calls me to come, He knows I stink. Still, it seems to me that He is grinning from ear to ear.

Time for my bath.

4

Following Your Passion

Making God Wait

*B*en is a made-up name for a lot of people who sit across the table from me and are as sincere as they can be.

"Pastor, I want to reach the lost and disenfranchised in the city."

"That's great," I say. "You are young, talented, enthusiastic and well trained. You will graduate seminary in a few months, and we can get started!"

"Well . . . you see there are these loans I took out to go to school. And I am thinking that God wants me to start a family soon. I am afraid that I will need to take a job with a larger church in a suburban community. Maybe I can support urban work from there. It has always been my dream to work in the city, and I was sure it was God's will, but . . ."

Gwen, on the other hand, represents those who go to the other extreme. She is in the city because God wants her to suffer. She is sure that any time she starts to enjoy life too much she is "operating in the flesh." Ministry in the city is perfect: Money is always tight, conditions are bad, and most people reject her out of hand.

No amount of conversation will convince Gwen that maybe God's will is that she operate where she's most gifted or that she's being rejected because, well, she's bad at what she's doing and everyone but her knows it.

Both of these extremes reflect a pattern of thinking that I've often observed in Christians and sometimes fall prey to myself. It's the notion that being in God's will means by definition choosing to do something unpleasant. In some cases, we choose something more comfortable and feel guilty. In others, we choose the difficult road and feel self-righteous. Not to mention miserable. We assume that God couldn't possibly want us doing something that we find enjoyable.

Instincts Good and Bad

*I*t's not hard to understand how Ben and Gwen reached their conclusions about God's will. Scripture has plenty to say about the dangers of trusting our gut instincts. Jeremiah declares, "The heart is deceitful above all things and beyond cure" (Jeremiah 17:9 NIV).

Perhaps the most notorious biblical example of the heart's deceit is David's attraction to Bathsheba. David was so devoted to the Lord that he is held up throughout Scripture as the ideal of a godly person. Yet he not only committed adultery, but murder because of his enchantment with this woman. Throughout that part of his life, he seemed blind to God's will and to his own heart's wicked desires.

Admitting this inability to see runs contrary to many of our cultural messages that say, "Be strong! Be the master of your own destiny!" The central paradox of Christian discipleship is that only the admission of complete defeat permits a life-transforming victory through Christ.

We have to break out of denial about our inability to see. Denial is a cloak of self-deception that blinds us and shields us from an honest assessment of our own dependencies and separates us from the will of God. Messages like, "I can stop any time I want to," or, "Things aren't that bad," are the kinds of self-assessments that dug David such a deep hole.

We may even project blame onto someone else, saying, "*You* made me do what I did!" While Bathsheba was culpable in her own right, she was not the reason for David's sin.

We might conclude from such examples that we're always on shaky ground when we follow the instincts of the heart. Yet David demonstrates another—and very important—side to the story. David's remarkable effectiveness as king was due in large part to the fact that he enjoyed his work so much. He found military life stimulating, he thrived on making administrative decisions, and he cherished the opportunity to be a spiritual leader of the people. While there were plenty of sacrifices to be made within the position, he relished the role itself.

Because the job reflected his temperament so well, he was able to pour his full creative energies into it. Saul, his predecessor, had considerably less aspiration to be king (1 Samuel 9:21, 10:21-22). His performance in that role was also much less impressive.

Think back over your life for a moment. Which teachers have had the greatest impact on you? How about the pastors or spiritual leaders? I'm willing to guess they've been the ones who found the greatest enjoyment in their work.

I attended several different churches growing up but was never greatly influenced by any of their pastors or teachers. Many of them, though not all, seemed possessed of a grim sense of duty and showed little zest for life. I wanted no part of such dreariness. But a few of those churches had an atmosphere strikingly different. Those on the pastoral staff were exuberant and took obvious pleasure in their work. Their enthusiasm was stimulating, and my spiritual life grew by leaps and bounds.

Those who have been the greatest help to me have almost always been those who enjoyed their work. Over a lifetime, we will each likely find that we most help others, and do our best work for Christ, when it's a reflection of what we most want to do.

And yes, the greatest risk, when you're passionately pursuing God by following your heart, is that you're going to end up misusing Him. You're going to end up using God and the church for your own purposes. But here's the good news, strange as it may sound: Somehow, God is okay with that. He allows for it to happen. Rather than fretting over the deceitfulness of your own heart, God would prefer you to trust Him to steer your passions, let you know when you've taken a wrong turn, and redeem even your worst mistakes (remember Solomon?).

Misusing the Church Building

$\mathcal{A}$nd, of course, if you're not going to worry too much about your own mistakes, it's probably best not to worry about others', either. Not long after I returned to church, I started doing outreach among homeless people in Boulder. There's an open, outdoor mall in the center of town where a lot of former hippies used to hang out and smoke pot with each other. In bad weather, it can be fairly miserable, but typically they're kind of stuck there. It's a great place to do street preaching. I'd pull donuts out of the dumpster behind the local donut shop, and I'd lay them out like a feast, and pretty soon a crowd would gather, and I'd start preaching and talking about Jesus.

One day, when the weather turned cold, I suggested we continue the conversation inside the church. "Hey, that would be great," everybody said. "We don't get a lot of inside time. Inside would be good." I didn't know anything about church, at the time. Somewhere in my head, I assumed they were always open all the time, so anyone could go in and pray. Makes sense, right?

We went over to the church building, but the doors were locked. Well, honestly, I don't know how I could have been so stupid. I couldn't imagine why they were locked, but I have some skills (the same skill-set I drew from when I was trying to get a hold of Kurt) that I utilized to open the doors. Well, if you can't imagine why they would lock the doors to the church, you surely can't imagine that they would have an alarm system. So we were all in the church, sitting in a circle on the floor having a Bible study, when the police showed up. I could have gone to jail that day, but the police were willing to call the number for the pastor that was displayed on the sign outside. They got a hold of him, and he vouched for me. He didn't know any of the other guys out there, but he knew me, and so I got out of going to jail. They just told us, "Go away and don't come back here anymore when the doors are locked."

The point is, I didn't see any problem with using the church to reach my own ends. I had decided what ministry should be going on, I hadn't checked with the church to see if it would be okay, I just . . . did it. It wasn't a horrible thing to do, it made for a good laugh, and it was motivated by my desire to preach the gospel. But, compare that to the story of Kevin, to whom I gave an opportunity to work for Trinity for a while as a custodian. One day, we had a bunch of stuff just go up missing, along with Kevin. Talk about using the church! He's still out there, and I still see him every once in a while. I wave at him as I go by.

Now, okay, Kevin looked as though he was using the church for inappropriate ends, and me, well, I was forgiven because I seemed to be doing the right thing, in my own warped way, but, in the end, we both misused the church. And I don't think there's any way around that. I can't stop bringing people like Kevin into the picture. Somehow, I still have to invest myself in broken lives, and if I do that, the church is most likely going to get used.

I'm still willing to use the church sometimes, myself, and even if it looks like, well, yeah, but Jeff's a *pastor;* he's using the church for *Christian* reasons, passion and sin are pretty closely connected. That's not a hard connection to make. In fact, sometimes we assume they're exactly the same thing. I don't believe they're *exactly* the same, but passion and sin go hand in glove. If you're passionately pursuing God, sin is almost certainly going to rear its head. Somehow, you're going to use the church to serve your passion. Somehow, you're going to use the people of God to serve your desires.

Pastors know this because we do it all the time. We grow big churches to fill our own egos. Or we grow pure churches for the same reason, and the smaller the better, because that just proves its purity. Either way, if you're passionate about it, and if you're not careful (or often even if you are), sin enters the picture, and the church gets used, or misused, both by people who otherwise might seem to have godly motives and by people who don't have such godly motives. Anybody who's passionately pursuing is going to end up having trouble perceiving the difference, and sin's going to be able to enter in. You're going to be capable—you yourself—of misusing God and the church, and I don't know that that's any different than Kevin the custodian ripping us off and going out the door, and maybe he managed to get high or used it to pay rent for a month, but if I can be forgiven, then maybe he can, too.

Tommy the Evangelist

My favorite example of this sort of thing is Tommy. Tommy is one of my best evangelists. When he was little, he didn't know a lot, but he knew his stepdad shouldn't be treating his mom like that, so he would stand up and say something about it. And at five or six years old, if you stand up and say something, well, you're going to get what's coming to you, especially if the guy is larger and drunker and more violent than you. Tommy got it pretty regularly. Likewise, out on the street, he knew those guys shouldn't be talking about his sister like that, and so he'd stand up to whole groups of them. And he'd get what you get when you stand up and they are many and you are only one.

By the time he got involved in Trinity's tutoring program the kid was a mess. You just knew he was destined for medication. As he was talking to people in the tutoring program, he heard the story of a God who stood up. This Jesus stood up against the many and then got what you get. Well, this sounds like a God he's willing to hang with. This is a guy who understands. And so he starts dragging all of his family down here, first his sister, then his mom, eventually even his stepdad started coming. Well, what do you suppose happens when all that brokenness gets brought into the church? At one point, somebody got knocked clean out on Easter morning because of a drug deal that had gone bad, and somebody owed somebody money and one of them was attending church here. Sure, they'd like to be hearing the message, and yeah they'd like to be getting better, but they don't all get better right away, and so the chaos is not just out there, it ends up (if you're doing your job right) inside the church as well. Welcome to the neighborhood.

But Tommy's evangelism efforts weren't restricted to immediate family members. Pretty soon, I'd start giving him tutors who weren't Christians. They'd be people who got involved because they were part of a literacy group somewhere and they just wanted to teach kids how to read. I'd bring them down here and give them kids like Tommy, and Tom would get after them about coming to church, "Come to church. Come to church. How come you don't come to church?" "Well, you know that's really kind of a personal decision, Tommy." Only Tommy didn't see it that way. Pretty soon he'd say, "Hey, I'm going to be singing in church, you want to come listen to me?" Eventually, they'd come to listen to him sing, and they'd all be standing around in church next to Tom, and they'd lean over and say, "Tommy, when are you going to go up front and sing?" He'd say, "I'm not going up front. I *am* singing." When I'd hear about that,

I'd say, "Well, you can't just lie to people, Tommy." But for Tommy, he had found a guy named Jesus who had stood up. He stood when they were many and He was only one, but still He stood. Tommy knew, even better, that He had stood for Tommy, and they killed Him for it. He didn't just get beat up, or abused; He got killed. This must be a guy who understands chaos. This must be a guy who gets it. And Tommy just wants everyone else to get Him, too.

Passion in Scripture

*W*hile Scripture has plenty to say about the evils of the desires of the flesh, it also brings out another and deeply encouraging aspect of human desire that has received far too little emphasis in Christian teaching. It proclaims that God himself creates certain desires within us who follow Christ in order to guide us in particular directions.

In Psalm 139, David talks specifically about God's guidance in his life and how it relates to his own aspirations. He declares, "For you created my inmost being" (v. 13). The term "inmost being"— literally "kidneys"—was a significant word the Hebrews used for indicating the personality. David is saying that God has given him a unique temperament and unique passions. This meant that God had put within him the inclination to enjoy certain work and roles. In speaking about himself, David conveyed a truth that applies to all people.

Paul makes a similar point specifically about Christians in Philippians 2:12-13, though our English translations often miss the full impact of his language. "Work out your own salvation with fear and trembling; for God is at work within you, both to will and to work for his good pleasure." Paul urges us here to make responsible decisions—to work out the implications of the salvation that we already possess. We should make careful decisions that accord with

God's will, and that will can be found, to some degree, within us, our desires and our passions.

Twice in the passage Paul uses the verb "work," which in the Greek is *energeo*—the root of our word "energy." Paul is literally saying, "God is energizing you." God is giving us motivation to do what He wants us to do!

Scripture pictures this process of energizing as one of the chief functions of the Holy Spirit. Jesus implied this when He termed the Holy Spirit a "counselor." (John 14:16) The Greek term meant a military official responsible for giving fresh courage and inspiration to soldiers who had lost heart in the heat of battle.

Interestingly, "motivator" is the most common role of the Holy Spirit in the Old Testament. When the Holy Spirit comes upon individuals, He gives them passion and fire to do what God is calling them to do—a far cry from the placid understanding of the Holy Spirit emphasized in much teaching today and in so many of our hymns.

We should expect, then, that if God is leading us to make a major commitment of our lives, He'll give us some passion for what we're undertaking. We'll be motivated for the task. There's something neurotically misplaced about the notion that we ought to follow the alternative we least desire.

But, you may ask, how does this possibly reconcile with the frequent biblical admonitions to deny our desires? Part of the answer lies in the quality of our walk with Christ. If I'm taking my relationship with Christ seriously, and making an effort to grow spiritually, I can be confident that many of my desires are being inspired by Him. I can trust, too, that many desires that I would otherwise experience are not coming to the surface.

However, this is only part of the answer. There is also a rule of thumb which is extremely important to understand. To best explain this, it helps to use the term "vocation" in its Reformation sense. Luther and Calvin used vocation to mean not only one's profession but any major commitment in a person's life. In their understanding, not only is my job a vocation, but also my family relationship, my involvement with my church, and any other significant investment of my time and energy.

With this in mind, here is a principle that should govern most of our major decisions as Christians: A decision for a vocation should be based as much as possible upon our personal desires. We ought to read them as a vital sign of how God has made us and wants us to direct our energies for Christ. But, in the day-to-day decisions made within vocations, we should deny ourselves in every way necessary to be an effective servant to others and to faithfully fulfill our responsibilities. Thus, self-denial takes place within our areas of motivation rather than outside of them.

When Paul speaks about the vocation of marriage, for instance, he stresses that much personal sacrifice and discipline are needed to be an effective spouse and parent. (Ephesians 5:21-6:4) Yet he also insists that we should marry only if our desire for marriage is strong (I Corinthians 7). So self-denial occurs within an area of life where we truly want to be.

Or consider Paul's teaching on the qualifications for a spiritual leader. In I Timothy 3, he notes many marks of self-denial and discipline that are needed by an effective "bishop," or spiritual shepherd. Yet often overlooked is the fact that he begins his instructions saying, "If anyone *aspires* to the office of bishop, he *desires* a noble task" (v. 1, emphasis added).

How many good, Christian people are convinced that "the office seeks the man?" They are sure that the more mystery in the process, the more certain it is that God is involved. The less you want to do something, the more likely it is that God is calling you to do it. Many hide the fact that they actually desire something in order to give the false appearance of this form of "righteousness."

Paul simply assumes that the good spiritual leader will be strongly motivated for the role. Self-denial takes place within that overriding desire.

5

To the Success that Follows Failure

The Gift of Homelessness

Six months or so after I started going back to church regularly, I lost the place I had been living in and found myself talking to a landlord inside one of his apartments. He assumed I wanted to rent a place to stay, which was true enough, but I didn't have enough money. I looked longingly at the apartment we were standing in, but all I was asking for was to rent a storage room for about twelve dollars a month. It was just off the laundry room and about the size of a closet. I really couldn't afford the twelve dollars, but it was better than having my stuff out on the curb.

How could this have happened? I was seeking hard after God, trying to do what He told me. I was shedding sinful habits and behaviors left and right, and my reward was to find myself homeless and unemployed.

I found extra time in the next weeks and months to study the book of Habakkuk, in which the prophet is praying that God would rescue his people, like He had always done before. Habakkuk remembered the old days when "His glory covered the heavens, and the earth was full of His praise. His brightness was like the light, and he had rays flashing from his hand." If God would miraculously step in then everything would be alright. A little miracle here, a quick wonder there. Manna from heaven, water from the rock. You did it before, Lord—do it again. But the answer God gave was not the answer for which the prophet had hoped.

"Look among the nations and be utterly astounded," God said. "For I will work a work in your days, which you will not believe." The prophet might have thought this was good news, but it wasn't. God was telling him that captivity and slavery, pain and heartache were coming. The prophet's heart must have sunk into his toes. Then God said, "But . . ." I love that word. The prophet must have leaned forward. This is where the good news comes, right? "But . . ." should be followed by, ". . . it won't last long," or, ". . . I will step in at the last second and rescue the righteous." Instead, all Habakkuk gets is, "But . . . the just shall live by faith."

Someone once wrote that the work of God is only built upon the ruins of the self. I'm not sure I like that much, but it is very often true. I don't know about you, but my times of suffering or heartache have always been the best times for growing in my faith. I asked questions, and God answered them. He stripped away what I did not need . . . my job, my home, my things . . . to focus me on the one thing that I did need: the knowledge that "the just shall live by faith." (Habakkuk 2:4)

I am not advocating being homeless in order to grow as a Christian. I am suggesting, though, that God is willing to allow times of suffering in order to challenge our faith and deepen our walk with Him, if we will listen. Sleeping on a bench means you don't sleep well. That, however, gives you extra time to remember the God who gave you even the bench on which you lie.

Habakkuk struggled with it for awhile, but in the end he was willing to say that even if there is no fig, no flock, no food, "yet I will rejoice in the Lord, I will joy in the God of my salvation."

Getting It Wrong

I'll confess that it wasn't the church in Boulder that got me all fired up about Jesus. After I ended my stint as a homeless guy by moving in with Kurt and Joel Goldsby, Kurt started inviting me to the Christian music concerts that were hosted by Calvary Chapel (under the leadership of Tom Stipe) every Saturday night in Denver. I had never heard of Christian rockers before, but if church didn't get me excited, music definitely did. Back then, these bands didn't get concert venues; they just traveled from church to church taking free will offerings. It was the early eighties, and the Christian music scene was just starting to explode. Everyone at those concerts was young, everyone was single, and everyone was excited by Jesus. Before long, it turned into a gigantic singles-shopping-for-a-spouse market. I'm not sure how that happens, but it's where I met Terri, so I guess these things can work out. I drifted away from the Church in Boulder, and started attending there so I could hang out in the same circles as Terri. In a few years we were married.

But listening to Tom preach one day—I'm pretty sure it was something about the rapture—I thought, "*I don't remember seeing that very well.*" And so I started really examining what I believed, really studying the Bible. I even bought a couple of books out of the Christian bookstore. As I read, I thought, "*No, I definitely don't believe that. At best, I might believe this middle position.*" I am sure that it was something ridiculous, some kind of slight shift over one direction, but what happened was, I started wondering, "*If I disagree with the pastor about one thing, what else do we disagree about?*" I started looking at what other church bodies believed, and the conclusion I came to was basically that some had good theology, even though their practice stunk, while many churches had horrible theology, and yet their practice was great. That insight was the beginning of my quest for a new place. Would it be easier to change theology or practice? Could I settle for one? Could I have both?

The first attempt was with a group of people (including Terri) who were already attending together. We were going to meet in a home, and all of us would be elders (even though, at twenty-seven, I was technically an elder to everyone else there). None of us had a clue, but each of us was as passionate as the other about doing the right thing. We thought it should be a group-consensus deal, where nobody would be in charge; no one would be called "Father," etc. If we couldn't agree on something, then we wouldn't move forward. We agreed loosely on what we would teach and how we would train disciples. We started coming together in worship, and we did our best to spread the gospel. We planned to start new places, and there was even some talk about moving to Alabama to start some kind of commune.

One of the guys, Joel, had a lot of family property down there. When we went to visit it, we passed all these porches populated with men who had nowhere to go and nothing to do. The whole place just stank of depression. When Joel pointed at a marker and said, "Well, the property starts right here on this corner," we all said, "Great!" but then we kept driving and driving and driving until I said, "Are we going somewhere else before we go to the property?" and Joel said, "No, we're going to the driveway." It was a lot of land.

The plan was that we'd all be working the farm, raising kids, doing church. Very similar to the beginnings of the Lutheran Church-Missouri Synod that came over here from Germany. They weren't particularly focused on reaching the lost; they were more concerned to protect who they were, and to keep pure doctrine and to start little German stores and little German farms and have a little German church in the middle of the village there near St. Louis. They were going to keep it pure because the government back in Germany had been forcing them to accept liberals and liberal doctrine in their church, and I think that, without knowing it, that's what we were doing, too. We were going to figure out how to do it right. It goes without saying that nobody else ever had, but we were convinced that we could succeed where everybody else (aside from maybe the apostles, of course) had failed.

Luckily, before we ever got as far as moving in to a commune, the church itself came apart. One by one people drifted off as they realized that not even the members of our little group were getting it right. We weren't mature enough to figure out that that was to be expected. By the end, it was just me preaching to Terri while she sat on the couch and listened to me reading from a set of old Charles Spurgeon sermons, each one about two hours long. Eventually I said, "This really isn't working, is it?"

It felt like a miscarriage. We had had this vision, this dream of church the way it was supposed to be, and it had failed. And I don't like to fail, even today, because I'm pretty sure I'm right. That's part of who I am, on both the negative and the positive side. Anybody who understood church planting would have been able to point out what we were doing wrong, but we knew so little. We didn't even know what we didn't know, and so it all unraveled. It all came apart except for the dream, the hope for something better, for a church that was doing the kinds of things that church should do, for a people of God who were being the people God called them to be. The first attempt had failed, but the hope remained.

Phones for You

*I*t wasn't long after that that I walked into the house and said, "Honey, God wants me to go to Africa."

Terri said, "You know what? That sounds like a good idea. Write me when you get there."

And I said, "Dang it."

Because I was ready to go. If she had given the nod, we'd have just left and hoped people sent us money.

Instead, I did a little preliminary investigating, and I said, "You know, if we go with the Lutherans, I think they're going to want me to go to school." I was twenty-eight by then, and I hadn't yet had a single day of college. "In fact, I think they're going to want me to go to a lot of school."

"How much school?"

"Well, they'll probably want a whole degree, and then I'll have to go to seminary, so we're talking, I don't know, six, seven, eight years."

Well, she'll tell you still, the only reason she came along is that she knew I'd never do anything for eight years in a row. She just knew I'd be coming back six months later with a new grand scheme, and school would be out the window. "But if you want to go to school," she said, "I'll come along." By now Nick was already born, the second of our four boys, and whether she admitted it or not, she felt like she'd have some control. At least she'd have veto power over wherever the Lutherans might want to send me. And Minnesota (for college) and Indiana (for seminary) seemed a whole lot safer than Africa and with fewer snakes.

So first I did a year at Front Range Community College in Colorado, because I honestly wasn't sure if I could pass college courses. I hadn't been in school since high school, and, well, maybe it had something to do with the drugs and alcohol, but I hadn't done very well there. Besides that, college wasn't very appealing to me. I couldn't imagine myself sitting in classrooms for hours on end listening to other people talk while I jotted notes. However, I passed my year of community college and started talking to Concordia College in St. Paul, where they told me, "Look, you've got to take Hebrew and Greek, and you can't get that where you're at, so you really probably need to come here." It was a good sales pitch; I probably could have taken Greek and Hebrew at the community college, but we took their advice, and we moved to Minnesota, where

I didn't always show up for class, and, even when I did, I rarely took notes. Still, the classes (at least some of them) were good, particularly the cross-cultural classes that I took under Dr. Paul Muench. The way the system worked, if you could get a professor to teach it, and two other students (in addition to yourself) to take it, you could get credit for it, so I'd make up classes and then talk people into teaching and taking them with me. In the end, I got a degree in communicating Christ cross-culturally, which I completely made up on my own. That was great, but I still needed to apply it. I was still searching for a way to do church right.

The area surrounding the college seemed perfect for a church plant. St. Paul, Minnesota had a broad mix of different kinds of people, different races and backgrounds. People from different lands speaking different languages. In one section of the city were people standing in soup lines, and a few blocks away were upscale restaurants where the clientele were requesting sea salt for their soup. I did the demographic work and a door-to-door survey and found huge percentages of people who were un-churched. I gathered some folks together to study Scripture. *("A good, solid core group,"* I thought.) I had professors from the campus who were willing to do the preaching for me and who were willing to still be there even after I left for seminary, so all the pieces seemed to be in place. Now all I had to do was gather a crowd.

Well, out in California I had attended a Norman Whan "Phones For You" seminar. Whan was a telemarketer out of the Friends church background, who had been involved in planting half a dozen churches on the West Coast. The plan was, you set up a group of phones and get twenty people a night making a total of twenty thousand phone calls. All the dial-ups are short: "Are you currently, actively involved in a church somewhere? If you are, God bless you, thank you for your time. If you're not, can we send you some material on a new church planting in your area?" And if they agree to get mail—we're not coming to your door, we're just sending you something in the mail—"Thank you very much," take their name and address, ring your little bell and say, "I got one." According to Whan, it didn't matter if you were selling Jesus or underwear, the statistics were the same. While there was something that didn't seem right about Jesus and underwear, I liked the idea. Out of twenty thousand dial-ups, you were almost guaranteed to get two thousand people, about ten percent, who would say, "Yeah, go ahead and send the mail." Then, once a week for seven weeks you'd send a different piece of PR material talking about, "A brand new church for all of us, where nobody's an insider; all of us are starting fresh, blah, blah, blah." After seven weeks, you'd call the two thousand back and say, "What do you think? Are you coming to the first service? And hey, if you are, would you mind bringing a dozen cookies?" Well, the cookie thing, of course, would hook them, even if they were going to wake up late Sunday and decide to skip it, somebody in the household would say, "Hey, we promised to bring cookies." Like we're counting on them or something.

Out of the two thousand people, you could expect about two hundred to show up that first day. It was like, just add water to your Chia church or something. You'd have to have a building, a pastor, and a worship team in place before the first person walked in the door, but I had all that, or I was confident I could get them. I was ready to start making phone calls.

But first, I went to the judicatory and asked for them to make me real. I didn't want to look like (though in reality I probably was) a loose cannon. I needed area church pastors to be willing to loan me some of their people. Their response was:

"Look, we can't afford this."

"But I'm not asking for money. I've got everything I need to get started. If you would just call this your church plant, I can go to neighboring churches, explain to them that this is for real and that, with the help of their volunteers, there can be a new church reaching people for the gospel in this area . . ." Now the man I was talking to shook his head.

"You see, in all likelihood, you will be successful, and you'll get a new church started. But then you're going to be leaving for seminary and the new church is going to need leadership, so they're going to come to us and ask for money to pay their pastor. In our experience, they will continue to need money for as long as twenty years. We can't afford that. We have plans for our own church plants later on."

"Besides," he said, "we did a survey in that area, and we didn't see any real felt need for a church."

"But I did my own survey," I protested, but it wasn't to be. Having asked permission and been denied, I had left myself with few good options. If the first attempt had felt like a miscarriage, then this felt more like an abortion.

Group Effort

Somehow, despite the church planting failures, I managed to finish college and move on to seminary in Fort Wayne, but I was starting to think, "*You know, maybe all I am is a lot of enthusiasm, and really I don't have a clue. Maybe I don't know what God wants. Maybe I should be back in construction.*" And, of course, all along the way people had been telling me, "You shouldn't be trying to plant churches, you should be focusing on being the best student you can be." And they were right. As far as I was concerned, I had work to do "out there," and if I had to sacrifice an A and get a B instead, I didn't care. In fact, if I got a C instead of a B, I still didn't care, because the deal was not, "If you get good grades, we'll make you a pastor," the deal was, "If I *graduate,* you'll make me a pastor." So I was just shooting for graduating. Well, that irritated them, I'm sure, but even with the overseas trips (I had been to *Côte d'Ivoire* twice in this time, alone as per Terri's suggestion, but I'll get to that later), people were telling me, "You've got a family now. You've got little kids to worry about. You can't just be bouncing around out there like some moron."

So, while the desire never went away for a church that behaved like a real church should, the dream seemed to be fading. Twice I'd tried, and twice, in two different cities, with two different groups of people, I'd failed.

And then I met a Pagan. There in Fort Wayne, I met Pastor Rich Pagan (pronounced păgăn). Rich was planting a new church, and he was going to use the "Phones For You" model to bring in a congregation.

I said, "Dude, I know how this works; let me help. Please let me help." I begged him to let me in on his team. "I'm here for seminary, they assign seminarians as interns to local churches. Get me assigned to you, and let me help you with this church." So they brought me in, and in planting Aboite Lutheran Church, a suburban congregation outside of Fort Wayne, a couple of things happened. One: We were successful; we gave birth to a worshiping community. Oh, it maybe wasn't everything I had hoped for in a church, but it was alive, it was growing, and it was reaching lost people. Two: I met Larry Merino, Randy Duncan, Steve Lee, and a few others who were there for the same reason I was—they wanted to reach people with the gospel by planting new churches.

Randy Duncan had a Jewish background, and we laughed about a Jew working with a guy named Pagan. Larry Merino and his wife, Linda, were gypsies who had left the Roma culture to attend seminary, and Steve Lee was a cop. It had been awhile since I had been in any real trouble with the law, but, to be honest, I still get a little nervous around the police. But there we were—a Jew, a gypsy, a cop, and a former thief working for a Pagan to reach the lost. That didn't sound like anything I'd read about in a textbook, but it was working. Aboite Lutheran Church was up and running and doing well.

About a year after we met, Larry and I were walking through a street festival in Fort Wayne when we happened upon a fortuneteller booth, and Larry started telling me about his heritage. Fortunetelling, it seemed, was at the heart of Roma culture, and when he and Linda had converted to Christianity and rejected fortune-telling, many of their family members perceived them as *gadjei,* or outsiders, foreigners. The gypsies think as poorly of the *gadjei* as the Jewish people do of the *goyim.* None of us should become one of them, and none of them can become one of us. There were even threats of stealing Larry and Linda's son Adam, so that he could be raised as a good gypsy boy.

Well, as a cross-cultural guy, I was fascinated. I said, "Hey, let's go talk to them."

Larry was reticent, at first, but reluctantly he agreed. He introduced himself in the Roma language, and they spoke of common relatives and acquaintances. "Your uncle Moyo once did me a great favor." "Your grandfather was respected among us." Then Larry said, "I'm going to seminary here in town so that I can be a Christian pastor someday." Well, that seemed a little odd to the people we were talking to, but, in the end, they said, "You are one of us. You must come over to the house. We will eat and celebrate your arrival among us." "Of course, I will come," Larry said, "but if I do I would like to speak of Jesus. Perhaps my friend Jeff could come with me, and if, after our visit, you want to hear more about this Jesus then we can arrange to start coming on a regular basis." I guess they thought that would be okay because the invitation was extended to me as well.

I don't know about Larry, but I was excited. We had just accomplished a successful church plant, and here was a whole new group of people who hadn't been reached, and who wanted to hear what we had to say.

Our visit led to a regular Bible study. The Bible study brought in new families, and new families brought us to what seemed like a whole new church. Forty, fifty, sixty gypsies and a few volunteers meeting in a home. The children were doing Sunday school in bedrooms, while adults were hearing the message in living rooms.

Larry, Randy and I went to Pastor Pagan.

"Rich, we know we are supposed to work with you for two years or better. We know we've only been here for a little less than a year, but we have this new church starting. It was only a Bible study at first, but now it's something more. Would you mind if we put our time into that instead of working for you?"

He was pleased. He agreed to be our spiritual covering, officially supervise us on behalf of the seminary, and turn us loose.

We called the church New Life, and it was beginning to look like a second successful church plant, then Nick Ziko, one of the gypsy elders, came to us with a question. "Have you guys read this passage at the end of the book of Matthew?"

"Which passage, Nick?"

"This one that says this is supposed to be for all nations."

"Where Jesus tells us to bring the Gospel to all nations. Yes, we know it well. So, Nick, what do you think?"

"Well," he said, "maybe this church isn't supposed to be just for gypsies. Maybe we're supposed to be telling other people as well."

It was revelatory for Nick, the idea of bringing non-gypsies into his gypsy church. It could ruin everything—and, in fact, it did—for the gypsies, but once the poor in Fort Wayne started coming in, I began to understand that this was more than just my second successful church plant—this was the beginning of God redefining what I meant by success, because, working with broken people, my own brokenness was rising to the surface.

I'm sure the brokenness was there in the suburban communities— it just wasn't as apparent. With a little money comes the ability to cover who you are and what's going on in your heart, in your mind, and in your life. Not to mention the fact that you're maybe not broken in the same sense that poor people are. The only reason you live in an urban neighborhood, often, is that you're not right. You're down here because you keep shooting yourself in the foot, and so you can't leave. There are a few people who move in trying to gentrify the community, but by and large, you're here because you're broken, and your brokenness is readily apparent to everybody around.

If you're working with these broken people to bring Christ and His gospel into their lives, you might assume that the gospel will elevate them, help them to see their world better and heal some of that brokenness. You might hope that they start to pull things together a little. But they don't. At least not right away. And so you end up with messy, bleeding, broken people all around you, and that's just the ones who stay. The ones who leave often make a lot of noise on their way out the door, and that can make the ones left behind feel all the more broken.

In the Celebrate Recovery program I have on Wednesday nights, I can guarantee that the majority of people who come in the door are not going to stay. The failure rate is always going to be larger than the success rate. You can't work with the broken on the street if you don't believe that to be true. There are some recovery programs that operate out of churches that have a couple alcoholics, a drug addict here and there, and since the Celebrate program talks about your hurts, your habits and your hang-ups, you can fill in the group with a lot of people who don't seem to be as oozing as the ones you're bringing in off the street. Your success rate gets a little higher, and that makes it a little easier to do. They are all just as broken as the next one, however and the failures end up wearing on you. There's a reason that only so many people can be in sales. It's because only so many people can take that much rejection and stay positive. Only so many people can take that many failures and still be okay with it. Somehow you need to develop the attitude of a baseball player, where hitting three out of ten pitches is phenomenal.

Poor people wear their messes on their sleeves. Broken relationships, broken lives, broken jobs, broken homes, broken connections to God and to one another. All this brokenness requires a response. You can't just tell people about Jesus. You have to wade into the brokenness. You have to be a part of the solution. There among the poor of the Fort Wayne community, I began to see a part of what I had been hoping for and dreaming about for many years. The church that I had hoped for—the people of God being the people of God amongst one another—was here.

This work took place with smelly people. You know, the kind of people you don't want to hug. People who were smelly in every possible sense, and I felt like I finally fit, like I was in a community where I belonged, among people who were admitting to themselves and the whole world that their life was out of control, and that they couldn't do it any longer. Smelly people, like me.

The Pact

Larry Marino and I were both grieving and celebrating at the same time. I honestly don't remember the specific incident, but somebody's life was broken again. It was a brokenness that we couldn't help with, a law issue, a health issue, or perhaps a relationship issue that we felt powerless against, and yet they believed the Gospel. They had heard us talk about Jesus, and they had said yes. Even in their brokenness. We looked at each other that night, and we knew that this was how life was supposed to be for us. Being there to offer aid to smelly people, or what we would call smelly people, was where God had called us both. We agreed then to hold one another accountable, that no matter where this journey took us, no matter what else we might be doing, no matter what else God might do, we would have this pact between us: *There will always be a smelly person in my life and in our ministry during our time on this earth.*

The constant draw somehow, is *away* from smelly people. I hold this up in front of God's people again and again. You can do ministry without them in your life. You can design the church so as not to be able to see them anymore. You could have an office and secretaries and staff who would work with smelly people on your behalf, but, no matter how you might justify it, smelly people would no longer be part of your life, and God has called us to the smelly.

He requires us to work amongst the broken and hurting. He needs us to be in the midst of one another's pain and darkness.

So Larry and I formed a pact: Whenever we spoke to each other, for the rest of our lives, we would ask a simple question: "When was the last time you hugged a smelly guy?"

More than twenty years later, that question still forms the basis of our conversations. Whenever we talk, we talk about what God is doing through us among the smelly people of the world. I'd like to make the same agreement with you. How can we hold one another up, pray for one another and be there with one another as we do work among the poor and the broken and the smelly?

Now, maybe you never thought to call these kinds of folks "smelly people." Some may find this offensive, and that is okay with me. Offending people is a part-time job towards which I sometimes put in a full-time effort. What I want to know is why you're not more offended by the brokenness in the world. I don't care if you're offended by my use of words and language. I want you to know that there are people dying and going to hell all around you. People you could probably see if you looked up from reading this book. People you can probably hear as you go about your day. People you live near, work near. If they are broken because they are disconnected from God's people, are hurting because they are disconnected from the holy, then they are smelly. If they are a mess because their relationship with God is messy, then we have work to do.

We had a guy coming into New Life who literally lacked any sense of smell. Consequently, as soon as the door opened, you knew he was in the room. It was just like, *Wow!* But of course, we were all too polite to say anything until finally, Larry took the guy aside said, "Dude, we gotta talk about fixing that odor!"

"What odor?" he said. "What are you talking about? What?"

He didn't know. He couldn't smell. It didn't bother him one bit. So he really tried after that to clean himself up. But I think there are a lot of people who can't smell their own odor, and so they assume that nobody else can, either. We have this tendency to judge success and failure based on whether or not we've got the odor cleaned by our own standards, but Jesus spent His time among smelly people. The Pharisees had fine perfumes and ointments to cover their body odor. The King, Jesus, spent His time with fishermen. The Sadducees followed the law to the letter and no one dared suggest any hint of brokenness or of falling short. The Lord spent His time with tax collectors and sinners. If you want to save the lost, I'm thinking that you will have to move over and sit in the smoking section.

6

Open Your Arms

Ivorian Baptisms

*D*uring seminary, I was still planning on spending my life overseas. The Liberian war was horrifying to those involved. In the midst of that horror I found an opportunity to be a part of God's work, in the midst of chaos. I had already spent one eight week period in western Cote d'Ivoire.

It's funny, the things you remember. One woman's hat from an entire sea of people. A baby crying. The wind was very warm that day.

It was my second trip to Côte d'Ivoire, and about two years after my pact with Larry. I was standing in the middle of the river between Côte d'Ivoire and Liberia.

My first trip had lasted eight or nine weeks. John and Kathy Duitsman had invited me to come down and train leaders, and I had taken Terri's advice and come alone. John and Kathy had been missionaries and bible translators in Liberia for twenty years. I spent a lot of time listening to them and hearing the stories. Then the civil war came and they went back overseas, this time to the Ivorian side of the border. The Ivorians they were among could speak French and

Krahn, the Liberians could speak English and Krahn, and somehow we'd get the message across to all of them, and then they'd go out and start churches in the villages.

The second time I went, the leaders I'd helped train had been doing catechesis in the villages for close to a year, and it was nearly Easter. The plan was the same as last time, except that Kathy had just gotten severely ill, so she and John had to go back to the states.

On the other side of the border Liberia was at war. Charles Taylor would send soldiers (many of them pre-teen boys) into a village at dawn to just start shooting. If you were fortunate enough to be living at the other end from where they began, you might have time to run into the jungle. No shirt, no flip-flops: whatever you were wearing to bed that night is all you had time to take. Everyone was running in different directions, screaming. Sometimes the screaming would abruptly stop.

Many ran east to Côte d'Ivoire. Most had never been more than five miles from home before in their lives. Now they were in a new country where a different trade language was used, and everything they knew was behind them. Thousands of people poured over the border looking for safety and receiving that, but little else.

The Liberian people had been hearing about Jesus Christ for years from folks like John and Kathy, but, well, you know, there had been farms to work and families to raise. Tribal councils and village elders often dismissed the Good News as being merely OK news—nothing to get excited about. There was life to live after all. But now, with no farm to work, no family to take care of, and no routine to keep people distracted, the churches began to fill.

The year before, all I had done was train twelve men to preach and teach. Now I'm standing in the river that runs between Liberia and Côte d'Ivoire. On one bank there is only bush and danger. On the other bank there is a line.

The line leaves the river and goes up the bank and disappears. People in the line sing, though softly, so they won't wake up anyone in the rebel army. They sing because in the midst of horror there is

God. They sing because one by one they are stepping forward to be baptized. Ten, fifty, a hundred, and still no end to the line, and still they sing. Two hundred, three hundred, nearly a thousand people will be washed in the blood of the Lamb and I must be in shock. The blood at work in the midst of bloodshed. The gospel compelling the masses. Even in the horror of sin—no—*because* of the horror of sin, there is something sweet and shocking about today.

While everybody's watching the other side, waiting for guys with machine guns to come out of the bush, I am standing in the middle of the river and baptizing with my right arm until it gets too tired and I have to switch to my left. Later, I will go to the next village and baptize out of a bucket.

For twenty years, John and Kathy faithfully watered, and then I showed up on one eight-week trip and harvested until I was so tired I couldn't harvest anymore. And it was just handed to me. I mean, sometimes you can fool yourself into thinking maybe you had something to do with it, but that wasn't even possible in this instance. These guys were just knocking me down to get baptized. It was the culmination of John and Kathy's life's work, but for some reason God decided to let me do the harvest, which is my favorite part. It was the pinnacle of my ministerial career, and I hadn't even been ordained yet. It was messy, smelly, and chaotic and it was all Jesus.

From Côte d'Ivoire to Cleveland

*B*y the end of seminary, I'd planted the church in Fort Wayne, started my vicarage in Detroit, planted another church that I'd left because it was big enough to bring the pastor in early, and finished what was left of my vicarage over in Côte d'Ivoire, where I wrote college papers about my experiences. Now that I was done, I was ready to get assigned officially overseas as a called and ordained servant of the church.

First, however, I had to go through a psychological exam. I suspect the doctor was looking pretty specifically to weed out guys like me. I was too type A, I would work too much, I would not support my family enough while we were over there, and in an overseas setting, if your family isn't getting support from you, they're not getting support from anyone. He was sure we'd all be back in the States receiving counseling in no time, and the church would have wasted their money, so he couldn't recommend that we go.

Well, the missions department had already scheduled us and two other families to go as a team. We were all heading to Canada for a year to learn French before heading to Côte d'Ivoire to help administrate and oversee these burgeoning little churches I'd helped create. Up until then, the church had not been legally able to admit I had even been to Côte d'Ivoire. At that point, they didn't have a volunteer mission force, so all they could say was, "If you want to take a vacation, Jeff, I guess that's okay," but they couldn't write and congratulate me on the success of my trip, because that would indicate that they knew why I was going over there, and if something had happened to me, they'd have been partly liable. So they went from, "We can't acknowledge you, but go ahead," to my asking, "Would you like to have a new church of fifteen hundred people in Côte d'Ivoire?" (and them saying, "Yes, absolutely we want it, and we'd like you and two other families to go,") to "No, not you. You can't go."

By this time Terri had convinced herself that Côte d'Ivoire was where God wanted us and what he had designed our family for. We communicate well with people of other cultures. She knew that I would be at my best there, and that we as a family would be at our best because of that. So she spent two or three days crying and washing the dishes because she wasn't sure what else to do.

So now we had to wait until the day of graduation to find out where we'd been called. They don't tell you ahead of time. I mean, sure, you've done the interviews, and you can give them your druthers, but that may or may not have anything to do with where you're sent. Some good friends, the Clockers, had helped us out with New Life in Fort Wayne the year before. They had two adopted black kids, and all Mrs. Clocker asked was that they go somewhere with an African-American population large enough that somebody there could do her kids' hair. She still hadn't figured out entirely how to do it, and she knew it would become more important to them as they grew older. Instead, the seminary sent them to Embarrass, Wisconsin, (no kidding). Well meaning people there would touch the kids' arms because they weren't sure black skin even felt the same as white skin. To quote those notable philosophers the Rolling Stones, "You can't always get what you want."

So I was disappointed, but not surprised, as I walked across the platform to receive my diploma, to hear them announce, "Jeff Johnson, Trinity Lutheran Church, Cleveland, Ohio." It didn't have the same ring to it as "Missionary-at-Large, Toulépleu, Côte d'Ivoire," but before long my disappointment turned to excitement as I realized that God was sending me to Cleveland fully equipped with a vision of planting churches in urban areas. There were all kinds of cross-cultural opportunities here that nobody had seen before, because nobody had been given eyes to see all the different people groups in the community. Had I known I would be sent to an American city, I never would have done all that cross-cultural classwork, and all that time I had spent planting churches among the urban poor had provided me with enough death and failure to be able to persevere through the chaos in spite of the smells arising from myself and those around me. God had prepared me in advance for a work I never dreamed I would want, let alone love.

Reaching the Lost and Trendy

ne of the first things that happened in Cleveland was that I got to watch God use a similar process of death and failure to shape the life of a young man (well, he was young then), named

Brian Upton, who is now the executive director of Building Hope in the City.

Brian had started in a church at a young age because his parents wanted to avoid busing so they enrolled him in a parochial school and the church at the same time. He had fallen away in college. Out in the work world, he had a good job and good friends, and yet, he was feeling a need to reconnect to the church, at least for Christmas and Easter, so he wandered into a traditional Christmas service I celebrated at Trinity.

What he found here was a church full of older folks who were very nice, maybe overly eager to see anybody under the age of forty walk in the door. In time they would become like grandparents to him, and they would treat him like a grandson, but what captivated him from the start was the vision of what the church could look like. While the rest of the congregation was saying, "Well, it sounds good, but we're really tired," Brian was saying, "It sounds great, and I'm not tired at all." In fact, God had been cultivating a hunger within him, and that dream of what a church could look like was appealing.

He and a few others in his age range came together around the question of, *What could we do that would be new, different and relevant, and that would serve the community well?* They were eager to build something, to contribute at the base, to make something out of nothing. They started worshiping more and getting involved in groups and activities with the neighborhood youth, and it was all very fulfilling, but as the millennium drew to a close, Brian in particular had a growing desire to see more people his age connected to this, or at least excited about it the way he was excited about it.

He had a degree in journalism and was working at an advertising agency on the East Side, a place filled with very bright, cynical, creative types with whom he felt very much at home. He was hanging out with them all day long, and yet, he also had a foot in this church that his friends found very strange. They'd say, "What are you doing, hanging out there? It doesn't sound like you at all." He'd say, "No, it's actually kind of cool, because this church is really trying to do something different." So that tension between working in this very creative, young, progressive environment and being connected to a one hundred and fifty year-old church that was very traditional and mainline eventually led to a decision (and to this day he'll tell you he doesn't know how in the world he ever agreed to this) that he would start a church that would be more approachable for people like his friends.

Well, it quickly became apparent that Brian's marketing job was getting in the way of his volunteer time, so he went to the management of the ad agency and said, "I'll work four, ten-hour shifts, I'll work four, twelve-hour shifts, but I need Fridays, Saturdays and Sundays off, because I need more time to pursue this passion of mine." They didn't like it, but they agreed to put up with it.

So now he had enough time to start some fellowship groups and to put together a little plan about how they would actually plant a service in downtown Cleveland that would be completely informal. Everything would be horizontal and organic—there would be no structure—but it would help reintroduce the historic faith to folks who had been turned off by the structure and the institution of the church.

Once he was committed to doing that, we asked for financial support to bring Brian on staff. He quit his job and started working with us full time, which was kind of ridiculous, really. He had been making good money in the working world, and his salary with us was about half what it had been at the ad agency, but he was single, he lived in an apartment, and he didn't have any really major expenses, so he figured, while painful, it was doable.

The next step was to secure a worship space. They found a coffee house that was ideally located in the warehouse district, just a few miles from Trinity. It's the hot and trendy (for Cleveland) area where all the restaurants and bars are. Brian approached the coffee house owner and said, "I'm guessing you're not terribly crowded at nine o'clock on Sunday mornings." The owner agreed. "Not terribly, no. Two in the morning, yes, but nine o'clock? Not so much." So he agreed to let Brian, who wanted to buy coffee for anyone who walked in the door (whether they came to the back room where the worship service would be or not), use the space.

Next, we advertised in the local arts magazine. These ads stood out beside ads for tattoo parlors, strip clubs and bars. I'm sure some people within the church community, if they were looking at that magazine, would have raised their eyebrows that we were spending good, church-people's dollars advertising in what they would consider a fairly smutty magazine, but it reached the target audience and people showed up. We had a new church plant filled with a lot of people on the periphery of faith. They were skittish as cats, trying to figure out if we were for real, but it looked like it was working. Then, four weeks in, Brian showed up Sunday morning with some other folks to do setup, and the coffee house had a sign up, saying, "We are permanently closed."

We would find out later that the coffee house owner had mob ties and was turning state's evidence, so his whole life had had to disappear overnight.

Needless to say, they were standing out there that Sunday, saying, "What are we going to do?" and "We don't know." So they came back to Trinity to set up a little ad hoc worship service in the school building here, while some of them stood out in front of the coffee house with pieces of paper telling people, "Here's where church is." They had to stand out there several Sundays in a row, because the ads were still running, and even after Brian pulled them, word of mouth had started to take over, and people might show up a month later and find the church was no longer there. It took several months to find another space, but they ended up moving into a cigar bar about three doors down from the coffee house. There had been a murder there, some hookers had been trafficked there, so it had been shut down. We leased the space, did another launch, and for a few years, it served as their worship area on Sunday mornings, and as our own coffee house on Friday nights. Acoustic music, art on the walls: It was a great space, and the whole thing was starting to seem like a resounding success, but around 2004, Brian and his team decided, "You know what? This isn't working." And they shut it down.

What they discovered is that we couldn't build an entire community out of a homogenous group of people. There was no diversity. They were all living downtown, they were all in their twenties, they all made a lot of money, and their lives were all very unsettled. So, in any given six-month period, this person would be relocated because of her job, that person would be getting married and moving out of the downtown area, while someone else would decide he wanted to be a Buddhist now instead of a Christian. When you have a whole church full of people like that, there's no gravitational center to make it stick.

Some of those folks are still in ministry with us, and that church did some good work, but after four or five years of trying to get it off the ground, its closure certainly seemed like a failure. But, looking back, we can see that, not only did it bless the folks that were in it for the time that they were in it, not only did they do some outreach trying to connect the Christian faith to folks who had turned away from it, but more importantly, it got Brian into a full-time job that allowed us to get Building Hope in the City off the ground. And you have to wonder, *Was that what God was doing the whole time? Getting Brian into full-time ministry so that he could become one of the key components of Building Hope, which is much more compatible with his gift set, anyway? Using this giant, painful experience of things not working to make that happen?*

As Brian himself says, "That was actually a really scary time, but what I learned from it was that failure isn't the end of the world. You know what I mean? I can fail at something and it doesn't have to define me. And it doesn't mean that God's not going to use it some way. I may not understand it at the time, but if I'm staying connected to Him, I'm going to see it bear fruit in some way, at some point." The new plant we called *In Search Of* was gone, but something equally exciting was being birthed in its ashes.

The Problem with Getting It Right the First Time

I feel kinda' bad for people who get it right the first time, who walk in the door and the first church they plant has ten thousand people in it after twenty years. Obviously, God picked different folks to do that, but how do you fight against the idea that somehow it has anything to do with you? That's not how it happened with Brian, and it's certainly not the way it happened with me. My failures did everything, including form my vision of what urban churches should be.

One way for the church to prosper in the city is this: Multiple churches scattered around the neighborhoods that people can walk to, that never have more than thirty to fifty, maybe one hundred and twenty-five people worshiping in them. Any more than one hundred families in a church starts to change the functioning of the church. Not in a bad way, it just does.

But one of the ramifications of that is that your pastors or shepherds don't get paid, or get paid very little. Your facilities are small and don't cost a lot for heat or light or rent. You'd probably need some larger spaces nearby where phones, copy machines, and support staff are shared, and maybe you'd have one professional who has all the education and leads the staff, pastors the volunteer shepherds, maybe coordinates some programs, conferences, or other events, but you can't expect everybody to be paid a living wage, because where will all the money come from?

When we wanted to bring Brian on board, I said, "We think Brian will be earning his own keep at the end of this, but we need seven years to find that out, so if can we get three or four churches, as well as the church at large, to throw in decreasing amounts of money over seven years, we (in increasing amounts) will pick up the difference."

Most churches, thinking in the old model, go to their judicatories and funders saying, "We're your mission down here in the city, and you should be paying for it. Just put us on your list and every year send us fifty thousand dollars." Well, that model isn't working anymore. Back in '92, people were just starting to think that through. We assumed it is a valid model. Maybe it was because of the cross-cultural and foreign work I'd done. Back in the seventies, people were writing about the three-self church (self-governing, self-sustaining, self-propagating) and later the four-self church (with the addition of self-theologizing, which is scary for Lutherans), but if it's not self-self-self-self, it's not going to last. So if I'm planting churches down here under the old model, they are always going to need somebody paying into them in order to keep them open. If that is true than eventually they will run out of funds. At some point, people get tired of giving money to this one thing; they want to give money to that other thing instead.

It looks to me as though we've got twelve, maybe fifteen years before the World War II generation will largely be gone, and that's the point when we'll hit a cliff as far as that model goes. The World War II generation is where we get the majority of our volunteers and money, and when they die, they're going to give their money to *our* generation, and *our* generation isn't going to give it to the church. We need to spend it on ourselves, because that's who we are. We need a lot of *stuff*. So the church won't be getting it anymore.

I'm pretty sure that our current model churches are going to see massive failure across the board in ten or fifteen years. And *I'm* still going to be here, so how are we setting ourselves up to deal with that?

One way is to build a big cathedral and invite ten thousand or one hundred thousand people, but what about all the others? Maybe one or two large congregations would be fine, but the church that I see is a network of smaller, house-church to mid-sized congregations scattered throughout the city, all connected together. If I did a hundred of those around the Cleveland area and covered all the different neighborhoods and all the different locations, we'd have a much more flexible model.

Our cities have a broad-based collection of cultures, anywhere from some slight (but internally significant) subcultures to communities that literally speak different languages, and you can't do one giant church in the middle of the city that everybody wants to attend, with one kind of worship and one kind of culture, because you're going to leave people out. Somehow, you have to balance the need for a sense of family and familiarity with the need for diversity and differentiation. You accomplish that, not by intentionally designing different cultures for different congregations, but by following the complex and chaotic process of listening to God, and by accepting the fact that, in this, too, you are likely to fail.

7

And Embrace the Smelliness

Listen

So how is it that we can step into this sort of vision and gain God's perspective for us and for our church? It starts, simply enough, with listening to the voice of God. The problem, of course, is that most of us don't hear Him audibly. In fact, we are a little, um, *cautious* of people who do. Nevertheless, it's the only place to start.

Listen to the psalmist describing the voice of God:

> The voice of the LORD is over the waters; the God of glory thunders . . . The voice of the LORD is powerful; the voice of the LORD is full of majesty. The voice of the LORD breaks the cedars; the LORD breaks the cedars of Lebanon . . . The voice of the LORD flashes forth flames of fire. The voice of the LORD shakes the wilderness . . . The voice

of the LORD causes the oaks to whirl, and strips
the forest bare, and in His temple, all cry "Glory!"
(Psalm 29:3-9).

How did God create the world and all that is in it? He spoke!
"Let there be light." And behold there was light (Genesis. 1:3).
Remember Elijah in the wilderness. A mighty wind, an earthquake,
and after the earthquake, a fire, but the Lord was not in them; but
"after the fire a still small voice" (1 Kings 19:12). Saul of Tarsus, a
persecutor of Christians and a zealous representative of the dominant
religious class, was struck blind on the Damascus Road. He fell to
the ground, confused and helpless, and then he heard a voice.

And then there's Sandra. Many people think Sandra is crazy. She
sleeps outside most of the time even though she has an apartment.
You can often find her standing in the middle of the street yelling,
pouring out her hurt, her anger, and her confusion for hours. Late at
night it can be frightening to hear her. Most people try not to listen,
and will go out of their way to avoid her if they can.

Because of that, they never get close enough to hear what she has
to say on her good days. I have found her to be gentle, thoughtful,
and wise, and if you can look her in the eye and really *listen,* you can
sometimes hear the voice of God.

You might accuse me of mistaking the passion and exuberance
of a psychological condition for the voice of God, and I admit that
I give preference to passionate and expressive people, but for me,
it's not an issue of whether or not God speaks through Sandra, but
whether I will get close enough to hear Him when He does.

I am convinced that God often speaks this way. Remember
Nick Ziko at the "gypsy church?" God speaking. Aliza's Dog? God
speaking. Tommy, my little evangelist? God speaking. Again and
again, God speaks. Are you willing to listen?

Scripture describes a God whose heart is set on communicating
with the ones He loves. Especially when you have followed a bad
detour, taken a wrong road or ended up lost through no particular

fault of your own, His heart and attention is irrevocably set on you. Listen. Can you hear it?

Refugee Work

I have gone through many periods when I wondered whether God was still speaking to me. I go to work and I go home. I wrestle with the bills and I help other people with theirs. The ups are all normal ups, the downs are all normal downs and in the midst of all the normality I start to wonder, *"Where is God in all of this?"* Maybe I'm really asking, *"Am I really where I'm supposed to be?"*

It was one of those normal days, or at least it seemed like it. The sun was shining and we were busy at the church. I was in another building when Brian answered the door at the office. Poorly dressed people looking for help is normal for us. Poorly dressed people with a lot of kids are not unusual either. This was different. A man named Francois Banyeretse, who's on staff with us now, was interpreting for somebody else who had been in a Lutheran group in a refugee camp. They had paperwork proving they were Lutherans (like we needed that or something, but it was important to them). They had been in the choir, even. When they arrived in the United States, they had started asking, "Where's the Lutheran church?" and nobody could tell them. Most people didn't even know what "Lutheran" was. Well, Francois agreed to help them look, because he could speak some English, and they showed up on our front porch asking, "Is it okay if we come to church here?"

"Well, sure," Brian said.

Their story was long, as such stories often are. There had been fear, flight, camps, starvation, and death. They lost family and left children behind. Throughout it all, they had followed God and prayed like Habakkuk that God would rescue them.

All the while, back here in the US, I had been in prayer. "Lord, we want to do more. All around us there are different people who need you. Poor and rich, black and white. Citizens and immigrants. What can we do? How should we start?"

I hadn't even been thinking about refugees. We now have this entire ministry that we actually have to rein in from time to time, so that it doesn't overbalance the organization. We could easily spend all our time, day and night, doing refugee work. The harvest field is wide and needs are huge. It may not be all we do, but man, do I thank God for the day when a bedraggled group came to our porch looking for the church.

It was grace alone that brought Francois, Kagoma, and their families to our door that day. Strangers in a strange land. New language, money and customs to learn. New jobs to get, and a new race to run, but in it all they knew to look for God's people. By showing up on our porch, they became the voice of God for us, giving us a new direction and purpose.

"Sure, you can go to church here," wasn't our final answer. Our response was, "It's great you're here, what can we do to help? And beyond helping you personally, let's consider something new and creative when it comes to meeting your spiritual needs." Which opened up a whole new can of chaos for us, but it led to another worship service, this time in Swahili. Francois preached half of the sermons, and I preached the other half. I'd give him some base material to work from, and he'd translate. Eventually that congregation had a split. A Pentecostal pastor who was starting a similar congregation showed up, and about half of the folks went with him, while half stayed here.

It wasn't but maybe three months later that the Pentecostal group came back to us and said, "We need to be doing some ESL work in the community. Could you help us?"

"We'd love to."

So while we're out helping that congregation, the group that stayed behind is down to about thrity people. After awhile we looked at them and said, "How would it work if we connected you guys to one of the English services? I'd want you to do a choir piece or two each week in Swahili, and in exchange for that, because gathering with people in your own language is important to you, what if I buy the goat, and we have a party once a month? We'll invite the other church, and all the Africans in the community. We'll have a speaker, food, and maybe some music. Not a worship service—just, well, African Night."

Their kids liked the English service better anyway, because they understood English fine and like most American kids they were tired of their parents' "boring service." The parents were thinking, *"Maybe I'll learn English a little quicker if I'm around it more."* They're proud of the fact that they'll still have their choir up there singing, and then, African Night, that's good stuff. Getting together is one thing, but having a goat and a party with all the Africans in the community . . . All this got started with two families showing up on our porch one day.

God didn't give us one set of instructions that we were to follow for all time. Rather, He spoke a need into our congregation and then provided the resources and insights to meet the need, even as it shifted and changed.

We don't have as many African refugees getting off the plane these days. Other refugee groups are coming now, in larger numbers. Whoever they are, though, when they arrive, we help resource them with volunteer mentors we've trained and screened. The volunteers meet the new refugees when they get off the plane and enter into a relationship with them.

I'm sure the refugees feel the same "God provides" thing that I do, because here these Americans are coming over to the house all the time, showing them stuff that you and I would take for granted. How to turn the stove on, what the refrigerator is for (and what it's not for), that you should be sitting on the toilet, not standing on it. Don't be afraid of the elevator—People are not disappearing. Basic stuff you don't need a lot of language skills for, but, as languages are learned, and relationships are formed over the course of the first year, people start asking, "Tell us about your God." For much of the rest of the world people aren't as afraid of talking about God as we are, so it feels quite natural to them to say, "Tell us about your God, and why you're doing this."

It happens. Somebody shows up and says, "What do I have to do to be saved?" or "You know, I'd like to retire and start working full-time as a volunteer. What do I need to do to do that?" And then you have to manage it somehow. Such opportunities come, I think, to everybody, but if you're not actively listening, they can easily be missed.

When I arrived and used what cross-cultural experience and training that I had to think through the different kinds of Hispanic people living in our neighborhood, I realized much of the church really didn't have a clue. Hispanic, to them, was Hispanic. It seemed to me that, at least in our neighborhood, the difference between Central and South American Hispanics, or between those with a Catholic background and those who didn't have a Christian background was larger than you could see at first glance. When a local Spanish-speaking congregation, which was populated almost exclusively by Puerto Rican people, needed a new pastor, the corporate church brought in a guy who was a former Catholic priest from Mexico. No big surprise, the church withered, because he did ministry like he was used to—He stayed in his building and waited for them to come to him for the sacraments.

The same thing happens with opportunities that show up for us. They may already have been there. When people walk up to the porch and say, "Can we worship with you?" a less passionate pursuit would say, "Yes, you can. You're welcome," and then, when they didn't come back, we'd have said, "Well, I guess it wasn't God's will." I'm sure we've done that ourselves in other instances. In that particular instance, it seemed to be a no-brainer for me. "Oh, look—a brand new worship service in a new language. I'd been dreaming about doing this. Let's go."

Arab Outreach

I was actively searching for this one. Who could I find to help me reach the Arabic-speaking people in Cleveland? I asked another organization, with ties in the Arabic world, to send me someone to lead it. Well, they kept sending me people who spoke Arabic but who'd never started anything in their life. They'd always worked for somebody else, had been teachers or chefs or something else. From their perspective, if they just did what they were told, filled out the weekly reports and followed the rules, they'd be fine, but I was looking for a missionary, an entrepreneur, a starter. I ended up rejecting four different people. All the while I was going back to them and saying, "Hey, how about Nick and Nadia?" and they'd say, "Nonono, we're using them for this other thing." I'd say, "Really, I think those guys could do the job." "Nonono, we need them for something else."

Eventually, Nick and Nadia were released, so I called them up and said, "Hi, I know you don't know me very well, but I'd like to talk to you about working in Cleveland."

We brought them on board, and they started an Arabic church in Cleveland. Two years later they got divorced, and the church dissolved, because in Arabic culture you need a man to run a church. Fortunately, Nadia is just as much a missionary as her former husband, so she's still with us, running a huge, burgeoning ministry among women in the Arabic community, and so the whole process continues to play itself out in her life, in their lives, and in our life.

It's not where I want it. I want a worship service. The women, by and large, can't openly go to Bible study if their husbands aren't Christian. It would mean not only physical abuse, but possibly even death. With a man to run a worship service, we'd have the opportunity to talk more directly to the men and get their involvement, but for now, there are a lot of Bibles and tracts stuffed in underwear drawers where men aren't going to be looking. They often sneak off to Bible studies, attend some of our events, and the work goes on. My life and this ministry is chaotic and out of control. Every new baptism I do, for a convert from the Muslim community, reminds me again that it may be out of my control but it is not out of God's hands.

Food Pantry

*N*ot all of our ministries are as dramatic as our work with refugees and Arab women, but they all tend to follow a similar trajectory. The food pantry that we run downstairs started because of the obvious need in the neighborhood. We felt like we should have *something*. So parishioners would drop off canned goods when they thought of it, and we had a closet for the stuff, and if people stopped by, our secretary, Elaine, would give them a little bag with four or five cans of food.

One of the neighborhood ladies in the community, who got some of that food, said, "You know, I know some people who work in shelters; maybe I could help you do a better job of that." She was a crotchety old Appalachian woman who always threatened to take her wooden leg off and beat me with it, but she stirred the pot and got things rolling. We gave her some space in the basement, and she took it out of Elaine's hands, (which was great, as far as Elaine was concerned). She has since gone on to glory and her daughter runs it now. I just assume I won't have to worry about that beatin' or her wooden leg when I see her next.

The food pantry, now serves about five hundred families a month. Most of the food is purchased from the Cleveland Food Bank for pennies a pound, and each family gets the equivalent of a couple days' worth of food per person. It's a big operation today, but it started with people just knowing that something needed doing, even though they didn't really have the wherewithal or the heart to do it right until somebody came in and said, "Thanks for the groceries," and "I could help you do this better."

The next step will be difficult, because just handing out free food is not necessarily good community development, so now we have to go in and say, "What we've done, we've done well, but how can we do it better still?" That might mean change for all the people who've worked so hard to get it to where it is, not to mention the fact that it's now sort of a family legacy, so it's going to be a difficult transition, but that's okay. We've seen enough to know that that's how God works. Chances are He's calling someone right now to step alongside the food pantry with a new vision for how it should work. We can only wait and hope that we all respond to God's voice.

Children's Ministry

few years ago, Brian Upton gave a talk at a suburban church about a Kids' Ministry we had started in a neighboring congregation. The two churches had once been connected, and we thought maybe we could reignite that connection. He gave them his spiel about how this other church was inviting kids from the community into their congregation. Not the kids who were already there, but the kids who weren't yet in church. At-risk kids, growing up in a rough environment, who need a place that's safe, where they're respected, where they can hear the gospel, get a decent meal, and learn how to pray. He told stories about some of the kids he had met through that neighboring church's program, and suggested that maybe they could start a Kids' Ministry of their own.

Pam had listened to his talk and taken his card before she left. Pam had a nice home, a wonderful husband, and a high-paying job as an executive in a local company. She could have stayed hidden behind all of those things, considered herself blessed by God, and called it a day, but she had been feeling for some time that there must be more to this Jesus thing than just going to church. More than neat and comfortable small groups that meet in each other's impressive living rooms. More than smiling and nodding at each other on Sundays and then going home to their personal pain and staying the heck out of everyone else's.

After listening to Brian's talk, she sent several emails to him along the lines of, "I couldn't sleep last night. Your stories kept me awake. The idea of what it must be like to be a kid in this environment . . ." and, "I'm a little bored with what I'm doing here now. I'm not finding it very fulfilling, but you kept me up all night with that story, and to me, that's a really good sign that maybe I'm supposed to be getting involved, even though I don't really know what to do or how to relate to these kids . . ." and finally, "I don't really know, you know? I don't really know what I should be doing, I just, I just can't sleep."

Pam not only got involved, but she ended up running the Saturday Kids' Program for four years. She got involved in the lives of at-risk kids and got to know their families. After awhile she had to make a choice. A lot of these families were not healthy. Even the healthier ones had a lot of messy behavior. This was going to have to be about more than leading Sunday school, or serving a meal. This would be much more than running a carnival or organizing volunteers. To follow God's lead she would have to become involved. Ministry in this neighborhood would mean learning new cultures, taking on new burdens and crying out to God for help. She would have to experience the endurance of suffering with others over and over again.

One child and one family at a time she keeps going. She isn't always accepted well. She gets trashed by urban people who suspect her motives, but she keeps going. She has cried with the grieving and partied at the celebrations. She still doesn't always understand. She shakes her head at the clothing or the music choice some days and prays about them on others, but she keeps going. Late nights, long weekends, and few boundaries tire her out, but she keeps going.

All of this has changed her, and not always for the better. Heartache and emotional scar tissue go with the territory. If you hug enough smelly people you end up getting some on you, but she hugs them anyway. She eventually transferred her membership to a church in the city, because she fell in love with the cross-cultural experience. She's still volunteering with us, now in a much higher level as we've started using her managerial experience more.

Passion and exuberance can sometimes be mistaken for the voice of God. Famous examples abound, from televangelists to the weekend shift at the local psych ward. God, however, is still speaking. To an unbelieving world that sounds crazy, but it is true.

Volunteers

*A*lmost everything we do relies on volunteers like Pam and the crotchety old Appalachian woman, and it can be tempting to think of them as free employees. We have a lot of people on staff these days, and they all need volunteers to keep their various programs and ministries running. We have to remind ourselves constantly that God didn't necessarily send them to *us* for the furtherance of *our* mission. We have to remind ourselves that one of our most important ministries is *to* our volunteers. It's just as legitimate an outreach as mentoring a child or teaching a refugee, so you've got to allow the volunteers to say no to one program because they want to try something else. The first thing they come on board to do may not be a good fit for them. They may end up hating it.

The important thing is that they've started moving forward into the task for which God is calling them, and the rest of us need to get out of the way and let God direct them toward who they are, what their gifts are, and what their calling is. We can't presume to figure that out for them. So while, yes, staff members may fight over volunteers, sometimes, because their program has to operate, the volunteer is in the driver's seat. If we can remember to be faithful to that, even when we're under the gun then we surely will see blessings somewhere else that will make up for any loss.

What God does to the volunteer is a mark of an organization's success and fruitfulness. Even though we work, often, in what appears to be an environment of scarcity—scarce resources in the church, scarce resources in the community—we believe, nevertheless, in a God of abundance, and he has proven himself trustworthy time and again.

8

Endure the Pain

Worship

*T*here is a story about Actor Tony Randall, famous for his role as Felix in the television series *The Odd Couple.* He was in a jewelry store in New York City. The store's owner recognized him and became very excited. He declared that Randall was his all-time favorite actor. What a treat it would be for his wife, the man said, if she could talk to *the* Tony Randall. Randall graciously agreed.

So the man called his wife, and Randall had a short, pleasant conversation with her as she gushed about how wonderful he was.

Finally, Randall came to the point of his visit. There was a gold necklace in the window that had caught his eye. He'd like to buy it. Would the store accept a personal check?

The store owner hesitated, and then asked, "Do you have any identification?"

Recognition only goes so far. The store owner was ready to idolize Tony Randall, but he wasn't ready to trust him. You see where this is leading, don't you? Is it possible for someone to worship Jesus—but still not trust him?

God speaks; we respond. God communicates to us and we communicate back to Him. It is that communication that forms the heart of worship. Sometimes, when we worship we feel a thrill, but worship isn't in the feeling. Sometimes in worship we gain a greater understanding of God's presence, but worship isn't there, either. Don't get me wrong—such things are definitely *part* of worship. When God speaks to us, we never want that moment to stop. Suddenly, the baby crying, the usher coughing, the sun glaring through the window—cease to be distractions because we long for more of God's presence. But worship isn't there. Not really.

> Take away from me the noise of your songs;
> to the melody of your harps I will not listen.
> But let justice roll down like waters,
> and righteousness like an ever-flowing stream.
> (Amos 5:23-24)

If you have a kick-butt worship band, and everybody comes and raises their hands and sings out really loud, and the offering plate is overflowing, and everybody is having a great time; if you have all of this but you do not have any sort of outreach to the poor, needy, broken, psychologically troubled, physically handicapped, or otherwise smelly, and you favor the affluent, pretty, smart, creative, educated, white, sophisticated, and otherwise resourceful and/or well-to-do, that isn't worship.

If we wait for a pastor who "never leaves a dry eye" or a musician who "can really get a group going," we're not putting our trust in the right person. Worship is not done by professionals at the front of the church, or in the balcony. Worship is the trusting response of God's child back to God in word or deed, in song or prayer, in high emotion or not. Worship "happens" when we listen to God and respond. It exists as we not only recognize His presence but trust Him enough to call back. It exists when we are willing to listen, and when we trust enough to do what we have heard. Worship happens when we turn and help the child who's irritating us in the middle of the service, when we give a cough drop to the usher or offer a prayer of thanks that we have enough sunlight to cause a glare on a Sunday morning.

But even more, it happens when the sunlight fails, when we no longer sense God's presence, and when everything around us is falling apart. It is in those times of darkness that our trust truly becomes worship, even when all we have the strength for is to simply keep showing up.

Eric Linthicum's Mother's Day Miracle

*E*ric Linthicum had served for almost seven years at St. Paul's, a semi-rural parish east of Cleveland, when the call came to move to Grace Church in Cincinnati. "I think I knew from the first telephone conversation that I was going to Cincinnati," Eric said. "I looked for the 'deal breakers' and they just weren't there."

To someone else those deal breakers would have been all over the place. Grace Church was in serious decline. Their former pastor had pled guilty to taking young boys to movies and buying them cigarettes—something along those lines—and about half of the church were sure there was more than that going on, while the other half defended him at every turn, because he was the greatest guy who ever lived, and he'd been a pastor there for years, but when he pled guilty to the charge of child endangerment, he was de-rostered and removed. At about the same time, a teacher at the school (who was also the principal's wife) died of cancer. The principal himself moved on soon after. Furthermore, their cherished German neighborhood was now eleven percent African-American and had a rising Latino and new immigrant populations. Urban life was coming to them, and few liked the idea. Several pastors before Eric had seen nothing but disaster and had declined the call, but Eric detected opportunity.

A passion to serve in the city blossomed in his heart. He accepted the call and got ready to move.

Everything seemed to be going according to God's plan until the day he preached his last sermon at St. Paul's. I didn't know him well at the time, but this is his description of what happened:

> "I preached my last sermon seven years to the day after I began my ministry at St. Paul's. That day, our youngest child, Hannah, just eighteen months old, was not her normal self. Instead of running around terrorizing people and disassembling the dinner tables, she just sat there. We thought, *'It's a hot and humid day, maybe that's all it is.'*"

> The next day, while everybody over the age of five was busy packing, we noticed that Hannah was still moving slow. We decided that, if it kept up, a call to the doctor would be in order. Tuesday, we called the doctor, who agreed that it sounded like nothing major, but she wanted to see Hannah anyway. On the visit, she ordered forced fluids.

> Wednesday, Hannah couldn't stand up. We took her to the emergency room, where she was sent to Rainbow Babies and Children's Hospital in Cleveland. On Saturday morning, June 5, 2002, (her nineteen-month birthday and the day before Father's Day), Hannah, my fourth child and only daughter, was pronounced dead. We went home and picked out the dress for her funeral."

They actually had to unpack their moving boxes in order to find a dress for her to wear in her casket; that's how close they were to moving away.

Grace Church told him, "It's okay. You don't have to start down here yet. Take the time you need to heal." But he didn't feel like he could. He had visited Grace and listened to a sermon that in his mind was ridiculous—lacking in any trace of the gospel—so he decided he needed to start right away.

Well, of course, it was a complete disaster. "During this time," he says, "I would sit at my desk and stare at the computer for an entire day. I was so depressed I couldn't find a coherent thought with two hands and a GPS. The new principal, the secretary, and some of the teachers carried me each and every day, and then I went home. Some times. Home was not where I wanted to be, so I looked for excuses to sit at the office." His wife wasn't in any better shape than he was, and, true to statistics, they got divorced.

I had attended his daughter's funeral, just to show some support for a brother in pain, so maybe that's why he thought of me when he tried to ask for help. He called me and said, "I've got this urban church that's struggling. They've got a school that has problems. Everything about us has problems. And I have no idea what I am doing. Can you come down and help me figure out what we should be doing?" Well, it didn't look to me like there was anything I could do to help the church, so what I did instead was spend about five years helping *him*, in the hope that someday he'd be called to a new church and have a chance to start fresh, because Grace Church was not providing a supportive environment.

It reached the point where Eric would walk in the building on a Saturday morning to find the church council meeting. "Hey guys, what are you all . . . doing . . . here?" They were having secret meetings behind his back. Even when he attended a meeting, they would restrict his input to opening and closing the meeting with a prayer. He had no input in the decision-making process. What can you do if you've got a church operating like that?

Finally, to cap it all off, he was given disciplinary action for proposing to a woman who was already married.

She's still his wife today, but at the time he proposed, even though she had been separated for some time, she was not yet legally divorced. She was in the process, but she hadn't received the official paperwork yet, and somehow this got back to the district offices in Cleveland. Well, after what happened with the previous pastor, the district president wasn't going to tolerate the least amount of impropriety, so he came down and told the congregation, "I'll help you form a new call list, and you can get yourself a new pastor." Eric was thinking he'd be lucky to get a job selling suits at Sears, but his congregation said, "What do you mean a call list so we can get a new pastor? Who said we're getting a new pastor?"

"Well, you can't keep this one," said the district president.

Well, the congregation didn't like the district president coming in and telling them what to do, so they said, "You'll not tell us when we need to get a new pastor. *We'll* decide when we need to get a new pastor." Eric tried to say, "Wait a minute, you have to listen to this guy," but true to form they said, essentially, "Shut up and sit down. We're handling this."

Politically speaking, the only option the district president had was to throw the whole church out for keeping a guy who's no longer rostered. He didn't want to do that, so he put Eric in a restricted status, meaning he could still pastor that church, but he wouldn't be eligible to do ministry outside of his congregation or to take calls to any other churches anywhere, for three years.

And that, it turned out, was exactly what Eric and his congregation needed. With Pastor Linthicum forced to stay, and his church forced to keep him, they had to learn how to communicate, how to work together, and how to form a new vision for where things were going.

Of course, things didn't improve overnight. More families left, and after seventy-eight years of ministry, the school had to be closed, but the turning point arrived on Mother's Day 2006, while Eric was standing at the altar praying in the middle of the service. First, he noticed an odor. Body odor badly masked by perfume or cologne.

Then he felt somebody rubbing his back. Well, knowing Eric (and depending on what he was praying for), he probably sounded kind of sad, and this homeless woman who hadn't been taking her meds had walked up to the altar to comfort him. The ushers were very nice to her and got her to sit down, but then, once the service was over, she went and stood next to him and shook people's hands like she was his wife.

Well, everybody remembered how crazy that was, but once she got back on her meds and started attending regularly, pretty soon they started treating her like *their* crazy, homeless lady. "Yeah, she's a weirdo, but she's *our* weirdo, and we like her."

And then she disappeared. The church asked around and discovered that the city had found housing for her, which was great, only they hadn't given her much choice as to where she went, and, for privacy reasons, they weren't about to divulge her location. Well, that made the congregation angry. Some, who had been most uncomfortable with her presence before, stood up and asked, "What can we do about this?" You see the pattern emerging? This was a congregation that didn't like being told what they could or couldn't do. Except that the city government just had. But in their powerlessness, something miraculous happened: they started to see that there might be more weirdos out there, and that maybe they could be doing something for and with those people.

One night, Eric walked into a council meeting and said, "Building Hope in the City is going to be starting after-school tutoring here at Grace on Thursday nights." Not "we are," "Building Hope in the City is." Never mind that Eric pretty much *is* Building Hope in the City down in Cincinnati, the church council looked at him and said, "Okay." He walked out of the meeting and said, "Wow, I can't believe that just worked."

Somehow, through all that pain and brokenness, they reached a place where they started seeing life outside their building as having something to do with what went on inside. Church and pastor began to work together more intensely and intentionally. The Cincinnati branch of Building Hope in the City was launched. They partnered with a sister congregation to help with a Kids' Church program. They began a small group ministry and, just a few months later, launched the Urban Family Learning Center. The UFLC, which began with summer reading, moved into tutoring and grew into adult education and ESL classes. A new spirit of excitement grew as they all started working together to share the gospel. Grace started getting visitors, and then new members, and then worship attendance began to grow.

A consultant for the Transforming Congregations Network recently told them, "You are aptly named as a congregation, for it is by the Grace of God alone you stand open and growing today."

Working through all of the grief and pain and mistrust is a slow and difficult process, and Grace has not had a big turn-around, mega-church style, but things are beginning to change. Church and Pastor are getting healthier and the wounds between them have begun to heal.

Back to their "Mother's Day miracle" lady. Pastor Linthicum heard repeatedly from members "Pastor you have been talking about urban ministry, but that lady made me feel VERY uncomfortable." Later some of these some of those same people came around and helped the congregation to engage in the same urban ministry that had originally made them uncomfortable! Recently one of these adopters met with Eric to plan her funeral because she wanted others to know the joy of urban ministry. She did not see her fifty-second birthday, but through her life and her family, along with many others, Pastor Linthicum and Grace Church have begun to turn the corner as a congregation and embrace who they have been called to be.

Resilience

I don't know about you, but the way God worked in Eric's life and in the life of his congregation causes me to rethink my own life and ministry on a number of levels. I have many days when I need to be reminded that God is there in the chaos with me, whether I caused it or it was thrust on me. It also reminds me that sometimes, "there's nothin' to it but jes' get through it."

There are a number of companies that make what is called, "resilient furniture." Simple, sturdy, water-resistant tables and chairs—not fancy in any way, but built to last. They're not cheap either; a plain white folding chair is about sixty to a hundred dollars. They're not as pretty as the office chairs I buy at a retailer for about the same price, but those chairs, as I am reminded every time I have to replace one, don't have a long life-span.

There's something to be said for basic, unadorned resiliency—the ability to get through, get over, and even thrive after trauma, trials, and tribulations. In this sense, sturdy beats stylish every time.

USA Weekend did a cover story a few years ago on the subject of resiliency, asking the question, "Why do some people bounce and others break?" The article noted that some people who experience trauma withdraw into a shell, while others, facing the same crisis, not only bounce back, but bounce back stronger than ever before. It mentioned that the topic is being studied in universities and taught in corporate seminars. Resiliency, the article said, could become the most important skill of the twenty-first century.

Researchers worldwide have documented the amazing finding that, when tracked into adulthood, at between fifty and seventy percent of "high-risk" children grow up to be, not only successful (by societal indicators), but also "confident, competent, and caring" persons. Most of us, it seems, are capable of being resilient. Emmy Werner, coauthor of *Overcoming the Odds,* says that this resiliency usually can be traced back to a mentor, teacher, or coach who "looked beyond outward appearance, their behavior, and their oftentimes unkempt appearance, and saw the promise."

Why do some people break down while others bounce back? Unlike furniture, I don't think it has to do with our design. A chair can only be as strong as it was made to be; it can't decide to be more resilient or less resilient. We, on the other hand, have access to support beyond ourselves. We have more than a mentor, we have a God who sees, a Father in heaven who knows us beyond our appearance, who provides us with what we most deeply need.

The psalmist cried out, "How deep I am sunk in misery, groaning in my distress . . . Why have you forgotten me?" Our perspective is important in times like these. The famous stoic philosopher Epictetus wrote, "Men feel disturbed not by things but by the views which they take of them." Psychiatrist Viktor Frankl, who survived the Nazi death camps, wrote that everything can be taken from a man except the greatest of the human freedoms: The freedom to choose one's attitude in any given set of circumstances.

"How deep I am sunk in misery, groaning in my distress." A depressing verse, but it doesn't stop there: "Yet I will wait for God; I will praise Him continually, my deliverer, my God" (Psalm 42).

Life is often different from what we desire, and events happen that we neither want nor cause to happen. Yet we believe that God is somehow present in our world, working out His purposes. Because of that, our wisest life stance is one of faith.

We trust. We commit ourselves to our God. And we invest our energies in the world trying to make it a better place. We believe that, although life is unpredictable, our God's justice, mercy, and love are always predictable.

Can you identify with the psalmist? Are you ready to give in and collapse under the weight of your sorrows? Are you asking yourself, "How deep can this hole be?" Time for the second half: "Yet I will wait for God; I will praise Him continually, my deliverer, my God." God has more for you, if you will wait for it. He knows you, and He knows what you need.

There's a verse in Philippians that is so often quoted its meaning is sometimes overlooked. Paul is talking about being able to face hard times as well as good times, and he states confidently, "I can do everything through him who gives me strength" (Philippians 4:13).

Resilience often comes down to a decision: Whose strength will I draw from—my own, or God's? One of the wonderful truths of the gospel message is that if you will look to God for strength, He will give it to you.

Cities of Refuge

*I*n the Old Testament books of Deuteronomy, Numbers, and Joshua, God establishes cities of refuge. Joshua 20:23 says, ". . . designate the cities of refuge as I instructed you through Moses, so that anyone who kills a person accidentally or unintentionally may flee there and find protection from the avenger of blood."

God established six cities. They were spread out for easy access, with signposts pointing their way. If a person committed an unintentional homicide, he or she would take off running. If the offender got to the city of refuge before the blood avenger tracked them down, they were safe inside the gates. After a time, a trial would be held. If the person was judged to be innocent, or if their penalty was paid for them, then he or she would be set free.

Time and again throughout my life, my passion (when it was not directed or channeled well) has led me into places I should not have gone. Hold any given scenario up in front of me and I am often capable of telling right from wrong and good decisions from bad, but in the heat of the moment, I sometimes rely on other resources than the Holy Spirit and good sense. I am overcome with wrong desires and motives, and I start to interpret these other influences as passion, and even passion for something good, like growing a church or "the ministry" and then bad things begin to happen.

Sometimes it doesn't seem to have anything to do with my decisions. Life or work or family or everything combined is turning south, and I feel like there is nowhere else to turn.

Have you heard some unfriendly footsteps in your life recently? Are you under enormous stress right now? Maybe you feel as if you're being tracked down, as if there are some malevolent people or forces that you just can't seem to escape. I want you to hear it again. Our God is a refuge-providing God. He delights in that role. He only asks that you avail yourself of the refuge that He provides.

Cities of refuge didn't mean much to the average person on Old Testament streets. But to the person who had a blood avenger hot on her heels, cities of refuge were the most important places on the planet. To those who know their brokenness and understand their need God's provision takes on a heightened sense of importance. Those who know they are broken have taken the first step.

Who needs a refuge? People who are oppressed or anxious; people who are grieving; people who are weary, disappointed, heartbroken, and lonely. People (in all probability) like you.

And yet, many of you just keep running and running and running. You may have read this far just to hear this: There is a city of refuge nearby, and the gates will swing open to you if you want them to. Listen to Psalm 46:1: "God is a refuge."

The first practical step toward accessing God's refuge is to call out and admit that something or someone is chasing you down and wearing you out. It's admitting that—unless you find a city of refuge, a hiding place, wings to crawl under—you're done. Defeated. Crushed.

God never promises that adversity will be removed from your life. But He does say that there will be provisions made for you to be able to walk a day at a time. His grace will be sufficient for you.

Some of you are facing such unbelievable amounts of adversity that the only way you're going to live above the line of despair is to orient your life around safe people and safe places and the refuge that God provides. A place and people who will accept you for who you are, and then challenge you to be more. Trust Him! He is faithful.

9

And Trust in God for Tomorrow

Repent

*I*t may well be that your life is out of control simply because the world around you is out of control, as well. Working down in the city requires a certain level of "madness," after all. It is in you, maybe even more so than in others, if you choose this life. Still, it is into this madness, this chaos, this stink that the God of the universe comes. It is here that He works, helping me to see my own chaos, admit to my own madness, agree that my life is out of control. It is only at the point of agreeing to my own helplessness that the next step can begin.

The prophet Joel wrote in chapter two:

> "Now, therefore," says the LORD,
> "Turn to Me with all your heart,
> With fasting, with weeping, and with mourning.
> So rend your heart, and not your garments;

Return to the LORD your God,
For He is gracious and merciful,
Slow to anger, and of great kindness;
And He relents from doing harm.
Who knows if He will turn and relent,
And leave a blessing behind Him."

Try to imagine people running through the city of Jerusalem yelling, "Blow the trumpets!" and the rest of that city yelling back, "What?"

"Blow the trumpets! Grab the shofar! We need to let everyone know!"

Can you see this picture? The people are asking each other, "Why? What's going on?" They know that the blowing of the trumpets can only mean one of two things: 1) We need to get ready for war; or 2) The leaders are calling a sacred assembly.

Eventually, the truth is learned—it's a combination of the two: War and the need to assemble. War with whom? Assemble to do what? The full impact of the alarm isn't understood until the verdict is announced by the prophet: "God is at war with us and we must gather in sacred assembly to repent!"

God's prophets blow the trumpet in our hearing and sound the alarm: "Wake up! It's time to get serious about sin. It's time to consecrate yourself to God. It's time to change your ways!" But wait—we're good church-going people. We talk to God every day and ask for forgiveness, don't we? Why another call for repentance?

Repentance seems so simple when you talk about it. The path I have chosen is going the wrong way. This is *my* path and not God's. I can just turn around and head back to the fork in the road. Instead of a left, I'll just take a right! It seems so simple, but in practice it is almost never that easy. I am far too often pursuing goals, vision, and end-results. Too rare are the times when I am pursuing God alone. Instead of following my Savior, my passion has been leading me and God has to stop me, rearrange my priorities and remind me that I am not called to be a leader or a visionary, or even a father or a pastor, but a disciple.

God also calls for repentance because too often we take it all for granted. There is a story, which makes me laugh just typing it, about the young private whose platoon was preparing for front-line action. Turning to his close friend, he said, "Listen, Charlie, if I don't make it back, and you do, would you take this letter and see that Sally gets it? Tell her my last thoughts were of her, and her name was the last word on my lips. And here's a letter for Jennifer. Tell her the same thing."

I like that story because I understand it at the core of who I am. In my personal chaos, I am a "two-timing" kind of guy. I know it, and God knows it, too. Through the prophet He is telling us to stop two-timing with the world, or three-timing with the world and Satan, or four-timing with the world, the devil, and our flesh. He wants us wholly dedicated to Him! He wants us to take the mask off, put our excuses down, and ask Him to "search me and see if there be any offensive way in me." Any offensive way. No excuses. No hiding. Do surgery, God, and take out the cancer!

Why? Why is this call for reflection and repentance such a big deal? Joel tells us that a "day of darkness and gloom" is at hand. The path we are on is not leading to glory and sunlight. What is the way to avert this tragedy and win this war? Turn back to me, God says. "Come with trembling bodies (v. 1), broken hearts (v. 13), and weeping faces (v. 17), crying out to the Lord for mercy!" God calls for an external expression that mirrors an internal reality—he doesn't want outward actions that are only a façade for lack of repentance inside.

The alarm has been sounded, but the trumpets only echo through the Judean hillsides now. What will be the outcome of a truly repentant heart, city, and country? Forgiveness! Can we be sure? Yes! God promises: "Return to the Lord your God, for he is gracious and compassionate, slow to anger and abounding in love, and he relents from sending calamity!" (v.13). What happens after the sin is confessed? It is wiped away by a more than merciful God who not only forgives, but also gives blessings abundant (v. 14).

Blow the alarm! Call an assembly! Begin a passionate journey back from your darkness and into His marvelous light.

God is willing to use adversity to help soften and guide passion and sharpen vision. The world, the devil, and our flesh all conspire against us and yet God continues to work, to call to us in our chaos. Into this madness, this chaos, this stink, He comes. It is here that He helps me to see my own two-timing ways, to admit to my own madness, to agree that my life is out of control. It is here that He calls for me to turn around and return to Him. It is also here in the madness and the chaos that He proves Himself to be a God who can redeem even the worst of our nightmares and begin to replace them with victory and joy.

Clean and Sober—Sorta

*A*nd then there's Fred.

When I first met him, not long after I arrived, Fred was probably clean and sober a full month out of every year, and then only because he would check himself into the emergency room and claim to have attempted suicide. Because he had a history, he knew the answers to all the questions they asked.

"Did you have a plan?"

"Yes, I had a plan."

"What was your plan?"

"To step in front of a car in the street."

"Did you work your plan?"

"Yes, I worked my plan. I stepped out."

"Did it work?"

I hate that question. If you're talking to him, then obviously it didn't work, but as once he answers "No," they have to admit him. He now has at least thirty days to give his body a break from alcohol, to get his meds back on track, to have some medical work done, maybe a little dental work, and maybe get a new pair of glasses. He'd spend January in the psych ward, padding around in his slippers and nightgown, and by February he'd be back on the streets, cleaned up, and ready to rock and roll. If he had it set up right, his Social Security check kept coming, his rent was paid up, and he'd be feeling healthy enough to go at it again for another year, or six months, or however long it ends up lasting.

Nowadays he'll be drunk only two or three months at a time, and it's been three years since he checked into the hospital. So he'll be clean and sober four or five months out of the year, now, instead of just one. Well, who's got the time to put fifteen years into a guy who ends up gaining only two or three months out of every year?

He's taken my new members class five times. Maybe six, now, but he's never finished it. He's expecting to be re-baptized, because he is sure he needs to be cleansed. While I disagree about his need for a new baptism, I do know that he's never gone the whole nine weeks without ending up drunk and back out on the street. He's been trying to finish that class for six or eight years. The six or eight years before that he wasn't even trying to start the class. He's maybe as close to finishing as he's ever been, and maybe we can get, this Lent, two consecutive month's-worth of clean, dry and sober out of him. Maybe.

Or maybe not, but that's what it means to enter into the chaos of somebody's life. "You know I try," he'll say, when he's drunk. "You know I try."

"Yeah, Fred, trying isn't enough."

But on the other hand, it's enough for us, for now. He is who he is, and you can either cut off your relationship with him whenever he's back on the sauce, and tell him, "Come back to us when you're ready to get right," or you can maintain the relationship no matter what and sort of trust God to transform his behavior eventually. I've consistently chosen the latter, but part of that may be me using Fred, and then Fred using me, and both of us misusing the church relationship. I feel better about myself because I'm in a relationship with guys like Fred, and Fred feels better about himself because he gets five bucks out of me, and I don't know what it is, exactly, but that's what life is down here. You take people as they are, and you continue to hold up where they maybe could be, and then you don't expect them ever to get there. You just keep moving forward and hope they (eventually) come along with.

The Men of Trinity

*A*nd then there are Bob, Nick, and Mark.

Trinity Church has become, for some reason (blame me, I suppose) a pretty masculine church. A lot of good-old-boy kind of guys have found it acceptable to be in this church. A lot of them came originally because their wives kept coming back, and they'd come to see what kind of cult she'd gotten herself into, but then end up sticking. Bob was a stereotypical biker, a hillbilly mechanic. He had been living in Cleveland much of his life, working in a factory. He is a good guy, nothing wrong with him, went to church with his grandma back in the day when they lived in the mountains. He says that back then you had to eat with your arm on one end of the table because you lived on a hill and your food would slide off a bit.

He showed up at church and, once he sticks, suddenly his kids are going to church because the whole family is going to do what Bob thinks is best. He and his wife Marion organized a Bible study and invited neighborhood folks. Once he got past his own suspicions about the church, he couldn't imagine anyone else would think it strange.

Nick was the same way. He came along with his wife. Once Nick got involved, the whole family had to get involved. He got a bunch of guys to go out monthly bringing blankets, clothing, sandwiches, and even hot soup to the homeless out where to the homeless lived, underneath the bridges, and out around the community, wherever the camps were set up, or where the individuals that we knew of slept.

We have a lot of guys like that who got lit up by that same passion that I was talking about earlier. These are everyday folk in all of their brokenness. When somebody like that gets started, the only thing you can do is get out of the way. Nick has since handed that ministry off to Mark Taylor, who's cut from similar cloth—been to church before, but perhaps for the first time he's lit up about what he believes, and now he's leading the ministry Nick started but didn't have the gifts to take beyond organized chaos. Mark's taken it another step further down the road. They worked together to bring the homeless in to be part of the ministry rather than just the recipients.

The Big Vision

*B*ob, Nick, and Mark are, in part, the beginning of what the ultimate vision looks like. As Moses said, "Would that all the Lord's people were prophets!" (Numbers 11:29). The ultimate goal is a city where the Church (not my church, not your church, but *The* Church) is in the center, economically, socially, and spiritually. I've never seen that vision come to fruition in its fullest form, but that's okay. It's not my vision, it's God's vision, and all I have to do is be open to the next step.

What does a city look like when its people are connected to God? There would be justice, for one thing. I'm not talking about forcibly taking money out of one person's pocket and giving it to somebody else, but you should start seeing that happen voluntarily. You should start to see money coming out of pockets without the government reaching in, or even if the government *is* reaching in. You should start seeing people practicing better hiring. You should start to see businesses thinking more about the environment around them—the cultural environment, as well as the green environment. You should start seeing people move closer to a better understanding of how we work together as God's people.

In the Swahili group, working as a people is well understood. A man stood up at a service after the announcements one day and talked about a problem he was having with his son. His son lied to get into this country, claiming to be twenty-two when he's really about fifteen. The fake age is on his documents, so he can't go to high school, but he doesn't look anywhere near old enough to be hired for a job. Nobody wants him, so he's started to drink, he's getting physically violent, and his dad doesn't know what to do anymore. In a standard Anglo community, people would say, "Yeah, that's too bad. You know the agency you ought to call . . ." but what happened in the Swahili group that day was that everybody stood up and started moving closer together. They began talking about what should happen, what was the right and good thing to do, and pretty soon we're all standing in this circle, shoulder to shoulder up against one another. Then they all look at me and say, "Pastor, what should we do?" Like I know. Pastors in our culture aren't used to people saying "Pastor, what should we do?" But the interesting part was that they weren't just saying, "What should *he* do?" they really were saying, "What should *we* do?" They were all ready to say, "I'm in, and here's how I'm in. This is going to cost me, but I'm willing to pay a price."

I'd like to see a neighborhood, a community, a city that starts to behave like that. So that it's more than just all of us going to church (although certainly we would all be worshiping together), but it's working together in the Old Testament conception of *shalom,* where people still do business, still make a profit, etc., but there's a greater concern for the community, and for the people around us, even to the point of others taking precedence over ourselves as individuals.

Some cultures, like most of the US, are very individual-first, where the collective or the group barely even comes into play. Other cultures, like much of Asia, are very much collective first, and individuals have to struggle to find out who they are apart from the group, and they're not even sure there should be such a thing.

I'd like to see some sort of whole, some form of the body where God's people within community are thinking in terms of the people of their community, so that the people, whether they believe in God or not, are looking at the church and saying, "Those guys have got something. I'm not sure if I'm willing to attach myself to it or not, but they've got something good." I know we're still dealing with sinners, but that's what we're shooting for.

When I was serving in West Africa, there wasn't as great a division between church bodies. If there was a Pentecostal missionary, a Catholic missionary, a Baptist missionary, and me all working in Côte d'Ivoire, we would all see ourselves as working on the same team in some fashion. We'd still have lines and boundaries but there we were all working together. We *had* to, for one thing, but we also *wanted* to. The air that those people were breathing out is what we wanted to be breathing in.

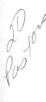

When I got to the city, I just assumed it would operate the same way. I was wrong. Our district president brought twenty-some local, Lutheran pastors together around a big table, and asked each one of them what was making the Devil happy about their ministry. That generated a lot of conversation. Then he went around the table again to ask them what was making the Holy Spirit happy about their ministry, and the best that some of them could come up with was, "Well, our doors are still open."

Once that was over, we talked a little bit about why we were gathered together. It was explained that we weren't really there to help out their respective congregations—we weren't talking about training their ushers or strengthening their evangelism team—what we wanted was to get together and do something that was larger than any one of us. Would it ultimately help their individual congregations? Of course, because people don't get involved in missions without strengthening the churches they came out of, but we're still talking about all of us getting together to do an "other" kind of ministry. 3 Pastors —

At the second meeting, three people showed up. As I talked about it with the other clergy during the next few months they kept saying, "Jeff, I don't have enough money for what we're already doing. I don't know how I'm going to give money to anything else. I don't have enough volunteers for what we're already trying to do, so how can I give them to anyone else? You can't get blood out of a turnip."

The world is not a limited pie. Building Hope in the City today operates with hundreds of volunteers a month in Cleveland alone, and many of them come out of those same churches that couldn't afford to have them go anywhere else. When the individuals themselves found out what we were doing, they came to us to get involved, and, for most of them, they're better members of their home church than they were when they started. About seventy percent of our budget is individual gifts, and all of those gifts came out of those churches that didn't have it to give, and I'll bet their offerings on Sundays didn't go down. In fact, I bet they went up. The problem is not that the different churches can't work together. We can't even work together within our denominations. We don't see ourselves as part of the whole, as a part of the body. One Lord, one faith, one smell.

The Vision Goes On

$\mathcal{D}$isney World had its grand opening in October of 1971. It had been seven years in the planning and over four to build it. As they were having the dedication ceremony someone is said to have turned to Walt Disney's widow and said "Isn't it a shame that Walt didn't live to see this." Mrs. Disney replied, "He did see this, that's why it's here."

Disney World is an impressive place. It has four different theme parks (Magic Kingdom, Epcot Center, Animal Kingdom, and

Disney MGM) on one enormous piece of prime real estate there in the heart of Florida. At forty-three square miles it is twice the size of Manhattan Island and among the top ten theme parks in the world. Millions of people continue to visit every year and have since its opening. All of this because of the vision of one man.

Vision is at the core of everything that we most enjoy. Think through any field (medicine, electronics, sports, government), and you will find visionaries at the headwater, the source of what we have for both good and not always so good. Our everyday lives are changed because of someone with a vision, or as Martin Luther King, Jr. said, someone "with a dream."

In the Scriptures, the word vision is used to indicate more than just a mental image of a better product or the hope of a different environment. Vision has to do with God communicating with humans through divine revelation. It is a word that occurs thirty-one times in the Old Testament alone and is key to everything that God's people have and enjoy. The Proverbs 29 passage even reminds us that without it "the people perish" (vs. 18). I am certain that this passage is so because God wants us to be about the business of accomplishing His plans and not our own. It must be His vision, His future that is kept in front of us or we have wandered off of the path and are heading to destruction. Course corrections on this journey of ours are both regular and necessary.

The people of Israel were on the very literal edge of seeing a vision that God had given them years before come to pass. After four hundred years of bondage under the hand of the Egyptians they had seen God part the waters of the Red Sea, destroy an entire army, feed the whole nation on bread from heaven. Numbers Chapter 13 tells us, "and afterward the people moved from Hazeroth and camped in the wilderness of Paran." The Paran wilderness was right on the edge of Canaan. They could see their victory, the fulfillment of the promise that had been made to Abraham. They could see the fruition of all they had they had been yearning for. No, I am wrong. They couldn't see it. It was right there. Freedom, victory, and peace, but they could see it and so they didn't enter the land but turned back.

Vision, God's vision, is more than passion, more than just wanting it badly. God's vision is more than mission, the plan for achieving. Vision, God's vision, is more than knowing or administrating or financing. Without vision, God's vision, all of those things in combination will not be enough. They can bring you to the brink, but stepping into the Promised Land will require more. We will need vision. We need God's vision because there will be obstacles that must be overcome and disasters that cannot be planned for. There is going to be discouragement and disappointments that we will have no control over. Thinking that we know, we will find out that we don't and assuming that we will stand we will see that we can't. If this vision we have is not from God it will not last and neither will we. Our passion will not carry us, only God can.

Here in the midst of the chaos, however, I can see something more than the desert that we inhabit. God is at work. In my brokenness and the ooze and smelly behavior of the people around me it seems to me that we are on the brink. I am certain that I can see it. Can you?

Epilogue

*H*elp me out. While there is no one right way to accomplish what God has put us here to do, we continue the struggle of looking through the chaos to find our way forward. Lives continue to be changed, though at a slower pace than I want. There is both success and failure. I can see God's hand at work in all of it but there is still a lot to do.

According to the New Testament, the world would describe the church by saying: Look how they love one another, how they care for one another. Look how they get into each other's business without being judgmental. At Trinity there are people who ooze with sores and brokenness. There are scores of people who, if you get too close, will end up getting some on you. The world is not gazing at us longingly, by any stretch of the imagination, and saying "Look how they love one another." We are as broken as the people who make up the body. Still, the journey continues.

As we work on figuring it out, some of us are caught up in micro-level ministries that deal with individuals and their needs. They are passionate and tireless people who are, often, riding the fine edge of burnout. We have a few people who wrestle with the macro-level understandings of urban work in areas like politics, economics, religion and ethnicity. These are all hugely complex topics in themselves and bringing any completeness to the conversation is difficult at best. Finding real life, ground level answers is even more difficult. We need help at every level.

Our ultimate destination is difficult to see, but somewhere in the hazy distance is a city built on a hill, a city whose center—socially, economically and spiritually—is the church. Not my church. Not your church. The Church. The body of Christ working together in koinonia to carry God's light and love into the chaos of smelly people who are dying for the lack of it. I want to see that place. I want to live a one-another life as it was meant to be. I want people to be saved, not just from poverty or illiteracy but also from sin and death. How does the local church in an urban area become viable missional communities of faith?

This "one-another" life we are all called to is about being in relationship. I know that is pretty messy but it's important so let's talk relationally. If you've read something that excited you, call me. If I made you angry, contact me. If you have suggestions, I want them. You can find me at www.buildinghopeinthecity.org. I know it can be better than it is, and I am betting that we can help one-another. We need new sets of eyes that would help us to see our city, perceive our call from God, and interpret our desire to transform our communities.

So, "let us consider how to provoke one-another to love and good deeds, not neglecting to meet together, as is the habit of some, but encouraging one another, and all the more as you see the Day approaching" (Hebrews 10:24-25). "Finally, all of you, have unity of spirit, sympathy, love for one-another, a tender heart, and a humble mind" (I Peter 3:8).

Have you hugged a smelly guy today? You'll know you were successful if you can still smell him after he's walked away, because that must mean he got some on you. Or maybe you got some of you on him.

To quote Nelson from *The Simpson's,* "Smell ya later."

*T*rinity Lutheran Church is a thriving, one hundred and fifty seven year-old Lutheran congregation located just outside of downtown Cleveland, in the heart of the near West Side. Since 1992 and under the spiritual direction of Rev. Jeff Johnson, Trinity has grown steadily in size and strength. From a group of fifty to a worshiping community of over three hundred, Trinity continues to reach out to new people and new neighborhoods in new ways.

Food, clothing, job training, tutoring, counseling, crisis intervention and recovery are only the beginning. Combined with evangelism, community development, the planting of new sites and outreach to immigrant communities, Trinity has become a place where people from many different backgrounds can now find a home.

The goal of Trinity Church is, through the power of God, to connect people to God and to one another.

Building Hope in the City is an independent Christian organization that was formed in 2003. Building Hope is about restoring the city to God by developing and linking people, communities and churches. We focus these efforts in four main areas:

- Urban Community Development and Church Planting
- Welcoming and Partnering with Refugees and Immigrants
- Equipping Congregations to Serve Their Communities Effectively
- Training and Deploying God's People to Serve in the City

Today, with a dedicated board, staff and hundreds of volunteers, Building Hope in the City's efforts stretch from Cleveland to Akron,

Washington D.C., Fort Wayne and Cincinnati. The organization provides a broad new voice for urban missions and for the importance of God's People to be present in the city, sharing His Word and their witness to His redeeming love in Christ.